T4-ACY-697

HAMMERMILL LIBRARY
MERCYHURST COLLEGE

Given in

Loving Memory of

Richard S. Cheney

art and nature: a series

old stone age

by Stevan Celebonovic

with a commentary by Geoffrey Grigson

Philosophical Library · New York

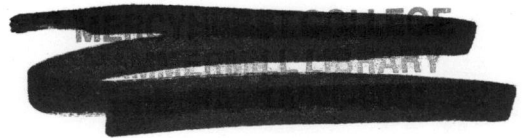

This work is copyright in all countries
by S. Celebonovic

Printed in Switzerland
for the Philosophical Library Inc.
15 East 40th Street, New York 16, N.Y.

At the end of the last glacial period, there existed in Europe a human population called Cro-Magnon. The origin of those men is unknown, their presence is an established, unusual fact. Some among them had the desire of modelling, engraving, painting apparently useless objects of their daily life. What was the sentiment which led those hands and induced them to create a picture out of inert material? The astonishing fact is that art appears suddenly and attains very quickly a very high quality. A new miracle of nature has thus been produced. Is it the movement of a body in space which, by becoming conscious, repeats itself and creates itself again? Which is then that state of conscience which starts art? Does it not indicate the birth of a new observing conscience, a rupture, a dualism: the outside world observed by an inner conscience? Is it the beginning of a personality? Does the mature man detach himself from the heart of nature like a fruit, like a being henceforth autonomous? And is not the creative gesture of art the nostalgic act of man desiring to be united again with that from which he is separated? Is art not only an observation but also a recollection of something hidden and, therefore, subconscious: life which man carries in himself and by which he is intimately bound to the essential of nature.

The ancients said that nature is the manifestation of gods. It is certain that art is the most intimate manifestation of man. There is a link between these two manifestations. A mountain, a valley, a river or the sea have a life of their own which passes beyond the elements of their components of life. Life is still that "other thing" which man evokes by his creative act and which therefore justifies the name which we have given this collection of photos: Art and Nature. It is not meant in the sense of an assertion but rather as a question.

We can only imagine the instant when, sombre and sonorous, space was born out of the non-existent. When movement had become possible in space, it gave way to adventure: life, form and other manifestations of movement. And its print, the form, tells us, like a very ancient chronicle, of that distant past. Centuries have past by, earth has changed its appearance many times in every respect and in every succession of size. Folds, eruptions and erosions followed each other. Strict and pure forms arose like laws, now and then troubled by opposite elements, discordant like passions. Hot climates advanced high to North and the ice extended periodically far South. As in a vast experimental workshop the material underwent a thousand avatars since the primitive life of seas, the tropical forests of the Palaeozoic, since the dinosaurs of the Mesozoic, the tiny mammals of the Tertiary and the rise of man in the Pleistocene. The straight line branches off into countless directions, rolling on a plan, extending on an axis and folding up in an egg-shaped return in itself in order to start off again according to its original rhythm. All these forms, limited by the possibilities of space, increase in number and riches. Manifold functions, ordering and merging, get hold of a form and, like a qualified agent, produce new possibilities, creating again simple forms.

But the most wonderful thing is that all these forms recall an echo at the bottom of our soul as if we had ourselves undergone all the movements of nature. These forms are in their expression a sort of archetypes buried in our souls. And when all that movement becomes really conscious and is created again in the human soul, we can then feel again the rhythm and the measure of growing. That awakening of the lucid conscience, before being reborn in pictures, passed probably through movements of the body—in dancing—and through the voice—in singing. The first artistic creation of man was the dull repetition of the movement of nature over the course of thousands of years. But without outward connection with the repetition, it is re-creation, it is expression of life.

There is therefore a consubstantiality between the soul of the primitive and the picture, and the rise of art is exactly its reflection. Thought gains in importance only at a later date and leads to the first writing in styled designs which is a branch of figurative art becoming a simple technique towards abstraction.

The Egyptians give us an example of developing figurative writing which appears probably before the first dynasties some 3000 years before our era, by leading from the imagery to alphabet. That evolution towards a more and more abstract medium of expression is based on the pure picture of the Palaeolithic. It will be sufficient to quote in that respect the parietal engravings in the grotto of the Addaura in Sicily. The lower part of the engraving which we reproduce (photo 72) represents a deer of the Palaeolithic, while the upper part represents two men who are probably being sacrificed, surrounded by several persons with birds' heads, reminding us of Egyptian stylizations. The Egyptian writing, on the other hand, has certainly served as a base for the Phoenician writing which led to modern alphabets, towards a form with a more and more abstract meaning. It is doubtless also interesting to note that, when the Egyptians used a writing called demotic which was already very abstract, the religious scripts continued to employ the hieroglyph writing. It must further be recognized that the hieroglyph inscription, where the writing unites itself with the designs accompanying it, lends to the whole a power of suggestion which, by other means, could not reach such a degree of expressiveness.

Starting from movement, extending to the fixed form of the picture, and leading towards more and more intellectual capacities, the way taken by the human soul is long. It ends in the autonomy of thought, in the detachment of man from nature " seen ". This seems to indicate that the Palaeolithic art probably corresponds with a function of figuration in man. Naturally, as a consequence, the intellectual faculties are becoming more accurate, and when magic is the result of it similar things attract similar ones and an important step is made towards clear thought. Is not the idea of magic eventually born from the contact of the artistic work which is already present and evoking? Can we suppose that the idea was spontaneously conceived by those who, at a given moment, made the imaginary jump by concluding that reality and figuration are tied together by intimate contacts, and that magic is the " daughter " and not the " mother " of art? Magic united with art has strengthened the authority of the artist and it is, therefore, possible that he has been the first magician, the first spiritual leader. He alone perhaps had the right to hurt the image magically with the medium of graphics, to draw the deathly arrow on the body of the animal, to wound it by that magic gesture before the hunters hit it in reality. But the art of the Upper Palaeolithic has to be considered, above all, as an opening up of the soul in the picture and as such it brings to our eyes the greatness and the beauty.

Stevan Celebonovic

Nature lay ready for Art—or for Man. That would be, I suppose, an old-fashioned way of expressing or describing the situation when man's consciousness, so many thousands of years ago, began to separate him more and more from nature and from himself—from nature and from sheerly natural man.

Nature and man have much in common: nature and art are always irreconcilable opposites and enemies, however much we talk, time after time, weariness after weariness, staleness after staleness, of poets, painters and sculptors—and town-dwellers—" returning to nature ".

To make something by "art" is to be conscious—with the consciousness, all the same (however acute), of man the animal. The purer this consciousness the better; whereas nature is appallingly unconscious and indifferent and impure. Nature is materials; is the flint, the bone, the antler, of the tools, weapons, carvings illustrated in these plates; is the pigments in which animals were painted on the cavern walls of France and Spain, is the flesh and nerve of the hand which mixed the pigments and held the brush, and is the actual limestone " canvas " of each wall. Nature is suggestion; is the hinting tone or shape; is the red deer or the bison or the wild horse out of which prehistoric artist-magicians, artist-wizards and wise men, consciously contrived images of desire.

Nature is full of patterns. There are wave patterns in a fragment of schist (Plate 1) which cooled from moltenness æons before men or hominids or semi-men first added point, weight and toughness to their hands by the provision of tools or made the first employment of fire. Nature—how extraordinary, if usual, to be still talking of nature as if it had a mind and a being and a personality!—is an amalgam of material and of forces fixing the pattern of venation in a leaf or the pattern of bark and branching in a tree-trunk. Having done so, and having no mind to care or admire, no will, no intention, no regret, leaf, tree and pattern are left by nature to themselves. The abandoned tree turns to brown coal, or lignite (Plate 2); an oak leaf as old, or as young, as the first arts of man, a quaternary leaf which fell from an oak in Switzerland in the warmish climate before the last spread of the glaciers from the North and from the Alps—bequeaths to posterity its print upon tufa (Plate 4) overlaid by glacial deposits more than 200 feet thick.

Nature is equally (and why not?) indifferent to ourselves, and our consciousness, our human artifacts and arts and images of desire. It reabsorbs and transforms traces of our activity. As I write I have in front of me a piece of breccia I knocked out of a shallow cave overlooking the Cantabrian Sea in the north of Spain. Brecciated shells, though, would be the better description. Each shell, each small limpet-shell, each top-shell still shimmering and blue and purple, was collected off the beach and the rocks below. Each shell was picked up. Each shell was held between a dirt-lined, rough-nailed, grubby finger and thumb. The soft inside was winkled out and eaten, and the shell then chucked clattering on to the huge midden in the vestibule of the cave.

How long ago? A mere seven, eight, nine thousand years ago, yet already each separate shell is tightly cemented to its neighbour by calcite, is reabsorbed "into nature"—whose digestive juices will no doubt prove powerful enough for New York or London, when it is their turn.

In Eastern Europe, witless natural activity, or nature, has piled thicknesses of loess, or blown glacial dust, over the bones of mammoths killed by palæolithic hunters, over the hunters' own skulls and skeletons, over their tools, over the fertility figurines, the Mother Goddesses or "Venuses" they carved or modelled, such as the tubby Venus of Willendorf (Plate 25) or the clay figure from the great mammoth hunters' station in Czechoslovakia at Dolní Věstonice (Plate 17). Utterly abandoned, never likely again to be caressed by human fingers the little enormous Venus of Willendorf lay in her Austrian cave under many feet of loess, from which she was extracted (in 1908) after a natural interment which had lasted the greater part of thirty thousand years. And in Western Europe nothing is more belittling than to see from a section at a cave mouth how nature has tamped down layer after layer of man's past (and nature's past), locking whole eras below a floor or floors of stalagmite too hard for a pick. I have in mind the Sacred Hill of Our Lady of Castillo in Northern Spain, a cone of flower-speckled limestone rising above a small spa; and in that hill of many caves and many prehistoric paintings, I have in mind particularly the threshold of the cave known as El Castillo or the Castle. Cut through by archæologists, the infilling of the threshold, under overhanging jags of rock, proved to be stratified with the horizontal neatness of a diagram in a book: here were tools, weapons, bones; the fauna of wet and warm and dry and cold periods; red deer, reindeer, wild horses, back to Merck's rhinoceros and the wood elephant which Neanderthal Man knew in the pre-glacial—or more exactly, interglacial—forests of Europe; back from vestiges of the brief historic Roman era, the first metal ages, and the Neolithic and Mesolithic phases, into and through the long extended twilight of the Upper, Middle and Lower Palæolithic.

-Lithic: Neolithic, Mesolithic, Palæolithic, New Stony, Middle Stony, Old Stony—our tool-making ancestor, our ancestor of art or artifact versus nature, dawns upon us chiefly as a fabricator of stone; and of all stones, of all the materials displayed by nature in front of his consciousness, chiefly as a fabricator of flint.

A flint hand-axe, Abbevillian, extracted from the river-gravels of the Somme, under thicknesses of loess and sand (Plate 3): how old? As a tool, a quarter of a million years; perhaps more, upwards perhaps of half a million. As a substance, as the sheer flint, from which the shape of the hand-axe was freed, by a man, the hand-axe is nearer fifty million years old; belonging to eocene years of vegetation above the chalk; to years, not before mammals, but before man. The vast ages go indifferently by, they pile up their debris, they bury their fossils, and continue in finer and still finer details the moulding and carving of the landscape; climate oscillates; and man evolves, collecting, grubbing, hunting, strengthening himself with tools, warming himself with fire, using caves where he can find them, scattering durable traces of himself thinly and less thinly above the earth from China and Java and Rhodesia to Europe.

He is an old hand at conscious processes by the time he leaves his Abbevillian hand-axe along the gravels of the Somme; and this album, plate by plate, now snapshots the sudden acceleration of his consciousness, or at least of processes which result from being conscious. "Sudden" suggests a hey-presto. But speeds are relative. To ourselves, accustomed to rapidity of change, invention and adaptation, accustoming ourselves in twenty years to more new materials than mankind had known in twenty thousand years, the flinty period of the Old Stone Age must seem at a lazy glance backwards nothing more than a huge and sluggish drag of time. Look back with a less provincial self-occupation, and the sluggishness, compared to the drag of man's previous evolution and his previous mental and technical development, and compared to the rest of life's behaviour, appears altogether mercurial and rapid.

Flint, that sharp, tough, shining, abundant and worshipful stone—worshipful since it was among the necessary determinants of our spiritual advance—gives us a micrometer of change. Wood vanishes for the most part, bone, according to the luck of circumstances, may or may not endure. Indestructible flint, though, remains to reveal a progression of technique. The man of Abbevillian culture may have been content with his hand-axe. However rough it was, however he used it and whatever the purposes it subserved, either held in his hand, or hafted, or thrown at his enemies or his quarry, he could repeat the shape of it at will.

Jump ahead—and it is a pretty long jump—to Neanderthal Man. Like the Abbevillian artificer he passed his term of life within the Pleistocene cycle of glaciations, the alternation of cold and warm periods marked by great glaciers snarling down from the North and fanning outward from the Alps, and then melting again. He began his European life in a temperate phase which cooled slowly to the last glaciation. If he was a savage, at any rate by the animal standards of his time, for all his low forehead and his beetling brow, and his slouch, he deserved Hamlet's praise of Man. There were plenty of brains inside his formidable skull (Plate 9). He reasoned, he apprehended, he was express enough, if not exactly admirable, in form and moving. Put him in a hat and suit and give him an umbrella (having shaved him first) and he would pass in a twentieth century crowd—indeed his type still occurs; give him glasses and he would pass around a conference table, or at an international meeting of learned archæologists. He may or may not have had a taste for cannibalism (which has not been unknown to his successor and supplanter and absorber, *Homo sapiens*); but he was an able huntsman. Apply flint as our micrometer of advance, and he was a far more accomplished artificer than the maker of Abbevillian tools. He still had a use for hand-axes; but he also adapted the flakes which divide from a core of flint when it is struck. From flakes he made points for spears—sharper than wooden spears of older usage. From flakes he made flint scrapers which were a step towards the pocket-knife in our own pocket. Excavators of his Mousterian sites (his culture is named Mousterian after the type site at Le Moustier in the Dordogne; just as he himself is called Neanderthal after the

Neander valley near Düsseldorf where a cave, in 1856, yielded the first fragment of a Neanderthal skull) have also discovered balls of flint which he perhaps combined into bolas such as were used in South America and by Behring Sea Eskimoes; joining them with thongs to throw at animals, so that the heavy balls, three or more at a time, would wind around their legs and tumble them to the ground.

Was he an artist, this Neanderthal Man? Can the measure of art as well as the micrometer of flint be applied to him? Much of an artist he may not have been. But why did he require rough pestles and mortars of stones (the pestle and mortar, by the way, is about the last item of stony equipment from the Old Stone Age which we have not discarded) unless he had colours to grind, natural earths, and particularly the red ochre of the limestone caves and shelters which he came to frequent as the climate worsened and the glaciers advanced for the last time? (Plate 7).

And why did he have colours unless he painted? Not, it is true, that he painted on cave walls; but nature provided another canvas, which has disappeared beyond all trace of hope of discovery—nature supplied his own back and chest and arms and thighs and face, his own skin, which, for ritual dances, may well have been the basis of Neanderthal or Mousterian art. Art from inside the head begins perhaps on the body, in patterns and symbolizations of red and yellow ochres, and white clay and charcoal; unless you call the hand-axe a work of art, as perhaps you should—not to mention all the lost articles of wood or bone or shell.

Images, purposeful shapes, were now, all the same, delivered out of substance. The opposition of art and nature, or artifice and nature, or consciousness and material, was now well established.

Yet Neanderthal Man was little prepared for eventualities. He had spread through Europe. He had reached the western sea-fringes. He was top man, even when a few other men with that neat familiar skull we carry with us upon our own shoulders had made their entry into Europe. He now survived from a comfortable, indeed a warmish Europe of leafy forest (in contrast to trees of the fir kind), from a continent in between ages of frost and snow, into the first millenia of the Last Glaciation, when the vast square mileage, tonnage, thickness, of the readvancing glaciers weighed down the land mass once more and lowered the seas, these glaciers having left us as their signature scratched stones from under their weight, and the scratched and smoothed rock-surfaces over which they crawled like dry slugs (Plate 10).

Neanderthal Man had known the wood elephant and Merck's rhinoceros and the red deer and the giant deer of the woods: he came to know the mammoth and the woolly rhinoceros and the reindeer of the tundra and the grass steppe. Warm winds had played around the wood elephant and Merck's rhinoceros, two creatures more or less smooth. Cold winds blew against the hairy mammoth and this woolly rhinoceros, who needed the overcoats of thick hair and wool which wrapped them round. Merck's rhinoceros held his head up and forward to pluck at leaves. The woolly rhinoceros snuffled over half-frozen ground, keeping his head and horns downward, to grub like a vast pig at a low, semi-arctic vegetation. In contrast to the wood elephant, the mammoth owned grinders (Plate 6) highly specialised to deal with grasses, moss, lichens—food tougher than leaves of the woodland.

Had Neanderthal Man lived too easily? Was he too leisurely, too conservative? In the "new" cold (new and sudden in our backward synoptic view) herds of game swept across Europe, and after them came new hunters in the first of a series of great East to West migrations—again, though now in larger numbers, men with the neat skull and more express and admirable gait of *Homo sapiens*.

It was the day now of this *Homo sapiens*: his techniques developed, like those of the Eskimoes, in face of a capricious, cold, tempestuous climate, his accelerated skills, and his ways of life gave him gradual possession of Europe between the ice and the Mediterranean. Neanderthal Man, like others before him and after him, had come so far to the fringes that he could go no further. He was stuck. North there was ice, west the immeasurable water. He could die out; he could be killed, or be absorbed, or both—in something of the measure perhaps that the Romano-British were both killed and absorbed after the shrivelling and disappearance of Roman power. From top man he became underdog; and disappeared at last; though something of him no doubt remains in our own physical and mental heritage.

Art, as much and more than the techniques of flint (or bone), now becomes the measure of the new invaders over many thousands of years until the melting of the glaciers and a transformation of Europe more or less into its modern style; and for a moment I am tempted to jump ahead in the sequence of plates to a couple of images (Plates 16 and 18) from the newly discovered and still unfamiliar Cougnac, which is a cave of wonderful delicacy and whiteness not a great way on from Lascaux and from the Dordogne, the capital area of the Upper Palæolithic in the west.

Who are the naked men stumbling forward in these two plates, in these two drawings in the cave, with javelins in their bodies?

First of all, they were drawn by an artist of the new hunter-invaders, an Aurignacian. Whether by accident or design the man of Plate 16 has been depicted, in black outline, across the outline, in red, of a *Cervus megaceros*, the giant deer, long extinct like the ancient European rhinos and elephants. The man of Plate 18 has been drawn, in black, across the red outline, not of a mammoth, but a wood elephant, *Elephas antiquus*. Both these animals of the leafy woods survived longer towards the South and the Pyrenees—long enough, at any rate, to be pictured in more than one cave in France and Spain by Aurignacian artists.

But these naked dying men?

I have asked myself, in the freshness of the Grotte de Cougnac, in front of these ancient drawings on a yellow wall, between twenty and thirty thousand years old, if the two men cannot have been survivors, no less than the wood elephant and the giant deer, into a colder climate and an alien world.

In other words, is it inconceivable that these two men, finishing a life nasty, brutish and short, may have been Neanderthaloids hunted down in the Cougnac neighbourhood by the Aurignacian intruders from the East—much as they would have hunted down any other game?

A safe enough question to ask, since no one can answer; and since this album is no textbook on the probabilities, dubieties and certainties of man's prehistory.

" The gambolling of lambs, however charming ", someone has said about art and nature, " is not yet dancing." The dance is formal and can be repeated. But is that enough for a definition of art—or Art with the dignity, for the moment, of a capital A? The tools of flint, which Neanderthal Man fashioned roughly with his rough hands, were formal; and he could repeat them. Were they Art? Are the flint tools or weapons to be distinguished as artifacts—artifacts, says the dictionary, are primitive objects shaped by intelligent direction—while the first drawings inside the caves of Western Europe are to be distinguished as something so altogether different which we define as Art?

Yes and no. Both weapon and drawing were useful. By drawing or painting animals deep in such caves as Lascaux, Altamira, Cougnac, El Castillo, or Niaux (Plates 46-61), drawing them, creating them, on the rock in pairs, male with female, and pregnant; and stuck with javelins or harpoons (Plates 49, 55, 61—and remember the hunted men of Cougnac in Plates 16 and 18), and caught in pitfalls or traps or narrowing corrals, the artist in his own feeling and conviction, we may suppose, insured the increase of animals as well as his own and his comrade's success against them in the hunt.

In other words the palæolithic drawing or painting was a tool, no less than the palæolithic object of flint or bone.

The drawings and paintings, no less than the other tools, were formal and could be repeated, within the limits set by the purpose which evoked them. Quite true that a second drawing, say of an ibex (Plates 15, 16, 19, 59) or a wild horse (Plates 22, 27, 54, 57) would not be exactly the same as the first one. But then a new hand-axe, a new point, a new scraper would not be exactly commensurate with others made before or after. Each, though, the repeated pictorial image, the repeated flint, would subserve its purpose; equivalent, in spite of minor differences. Each in its class would be equally useful, as animal image, as weapon to be employed against animals or on their carcases.

So, in a way, that Art Something which we sophisticatedly distinguish as a primary quality, was secondary to this sheer making for a purpose. It is really a distinction, or different degree, of an intensity which has been transferred from man to object. The Upper Palæolithic "artist" puts more of the intensity and energy and scope of the Upper Palæolithic mind and life into his drawing of an animal than he needs to put into the careful fashioning of a point or a scraper. After all, his life narrowed to intensities of desire over mammoth, ibex, wild horse, red deer, bison, and wild cattle. Give us this Day our Daily Bread: the game he subdued was light, warmth, food, clothing, and material for a dozen other necessities. So as well as passionately desiring a fertile abundance of the animals he hunted, he could also feel a kinship with them, and a sacramentality about their existence (have you noticed how a modern M.F.H. shows a kind of vestigial or atavistic love for the fox?).

The sacramentality gets into this sacramental tool, this drawing in the cave. The hunter-artist, the artist-magician, is not content with a schematic scrawl. He draws his selected animals—the Art Something more and more emphasized—with purer and purer grace of outline, stronger and stronger rhythm. Why? Because he loves and admires what he is drawing. *Chi pingere figura, si non può esser lei, non la può porre*: " Who paints a figure, if he cannot be it, cannot draw it." The early artist gives himself intensely, energetically to the animal he draws, to its grace, to its contours: he *is* the animal he draws.

In any case, he responds as a man to rhythm and proportion; and strives for the best rhythm and the best proportion in satisfaction of his own mental ease and comfort; which is the difference between the emotional effects of shape and shapelessness, between the path or pavement and the helter-skelter of fallen stones, between the star-gazer's selected arbitrary constellations and the unrhythmical mess of stars in the black sky.

Note that the Palæolithic artist as a general rule draws images of men, who are not so much targets of his intensest projection (he takes them for granted), with far less interest, love and similitude. Thousands of years on he was to take to a Magdalenian portraiture or at any rate depiction of human heads, as upon the slabs of stone found in 1937 in the Grotte de la Marche, in Lussac-les-Châteaux. But to begin with and through most of the Upper Palæolithic era, he turns man, when he has occasion to draw him at all, into an almost featureless, or actually featureless manikin, or into a masked manikin—as, for example, upon those sparkling walls of Cougnac. Before condemning this as primeval barbarism, remember the great Claude Lorraine; he was a dab at painting the light and landscape and trees and rocks he loved, a dolt at the cattle or men he felt he had to insert.

Where, though, was the beginning? The actual beginning of "art" —of artifact, at least, permeated with that extra Something, that extra energy and feeling, which distinguished it from the hand-axe? In prehistory it seems we have to answer separately for the complex of sculpture and for the pictorial complex of drawing, engraving and painting. They overlap, they fuse, before the forests return across Europe and the Old Stone Age comes to an end. But broadly the pictorial complex seems to have begun with the culture or peoples archæologically labelled "Aurignacian", while the sculptural complex began with the culture or peoples labelled nowadays "Gravettian".

Aurignacians launch the principal migrations into Europe. The evidence—wherever in fact their Asiatic home had been—suggests a people used to hilly country or the neighbourhood of mountains, and used to sheltering in caves or more exactly sheltering below overhangs of rock, the *abris* of the French archæologist, the rock-shelters open to the light, dry, easily made less draughty and more weatherproof with stones or skins and branches, giving the hunters safety at their backs and overhead, and a wide view in front of them and (very often) below.

These Aurignacian incomers were much on the move, collectors of food as well as hunters. They followed the game, semi-nomads on a more or less regular time-table and itinerary through the year; which would allow them to return, for the colder winter, to their favourite *abris*, not to mention the deeper caverns in which they were already making their first ritual drawings, their first animal images.

If the record of the caverns is rightly interpreted, then in the depth of one shrine and another in France and Northern Spain—in Altamira, El Castillo, Gargas and Pech-Merle, for example—it is possible to trace a development of technique and expressive ability for the pictorial complex of art.

Apes have been observed to trace the outline of their hands upon the ground. Aurignacians made prints or stencils of their hands in their ritual caverns. Gargas, in the Pyrenean foothills, is above all the Cave of the Hands, a damp roomy cave, with " gours " or rimstone pools on the floor; and hand-and-finger stencils surrounded with patches of red ochre on the walls—some of them of mutilated hands. The damp ochre patches glow in the electric light of the cave.

Fingers, though, are tools; and they itch for activity on their own—formative or creative activity. The early Aurignacians did not confine themselves to blowing pigment from their mouths or from a hollow bone aound fingers spread idly and inactively upon the limestone. With those same fingers they scrawled images on the clay. In many caves (Gargas is one of them) a thin deposit of clay covers some part of wall or roof, lying ready and inviting like the wax of Roman tablets. Aurignacians scrawled their meander shapes and images in this clay: their desires came to the tips of their fingers. In this meander or macaroni technique they scrawled outlines of animals and the crudest outlines of men and women. (After fingers, bones and sticks were used as the stylus.)

Techniques coalesce into new suggestion, and combine into new techniques. The Upper Palæolithic hunter paints his body, let us suppose, much as the Black Fellow of Australia paints his skin for the corroberee: he lays his hand for steadiness on the ground, on a boulder, then

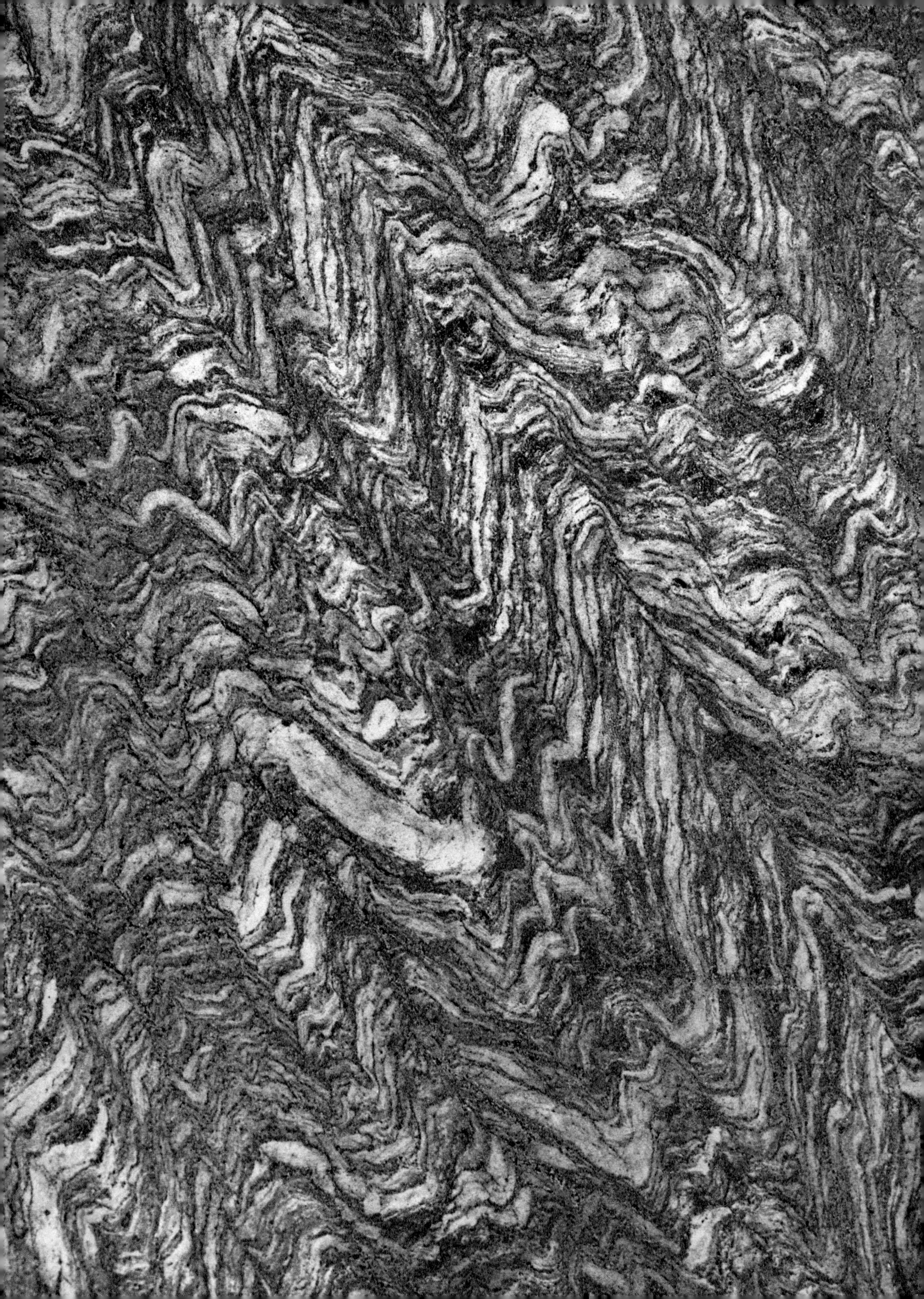

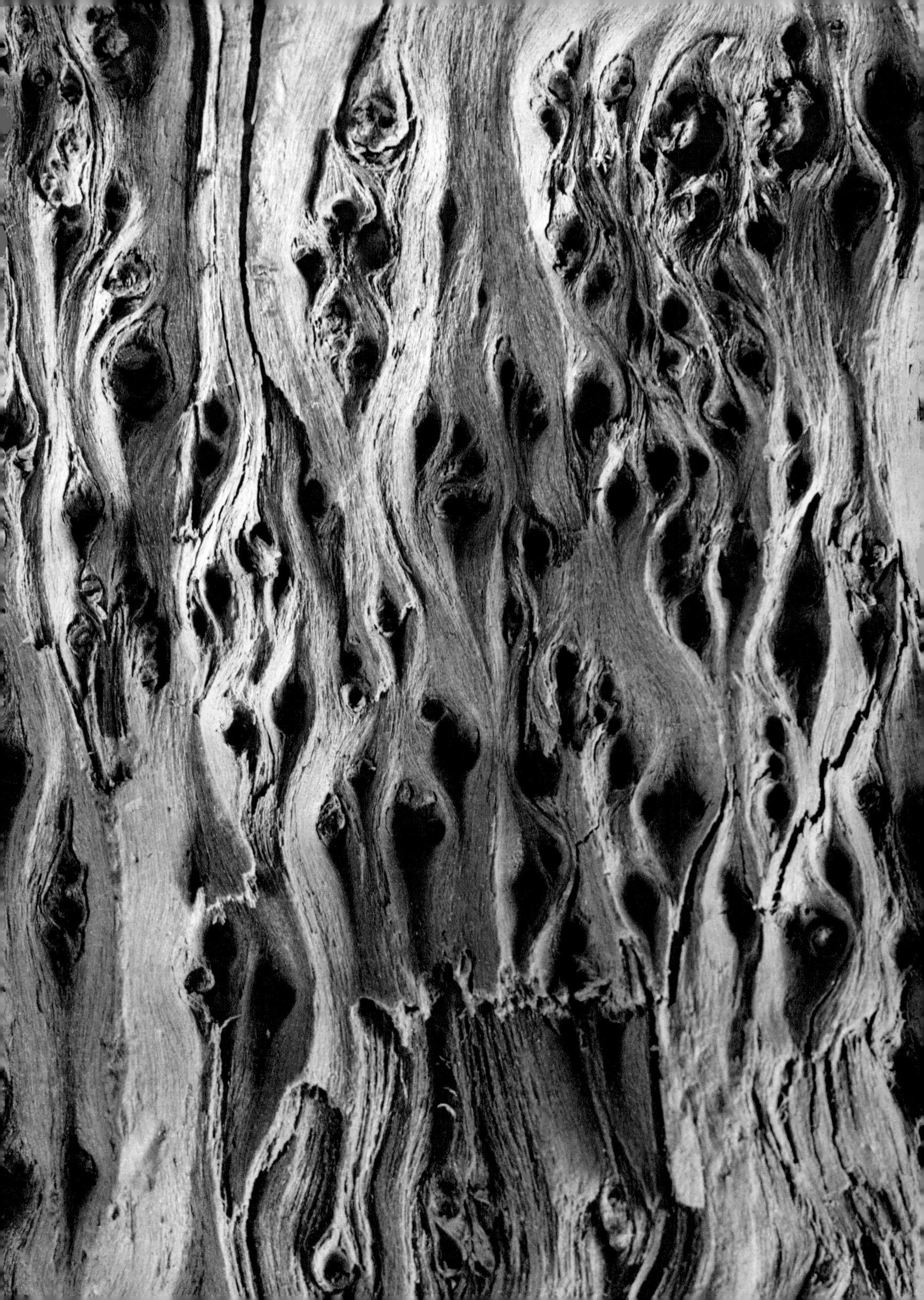

3

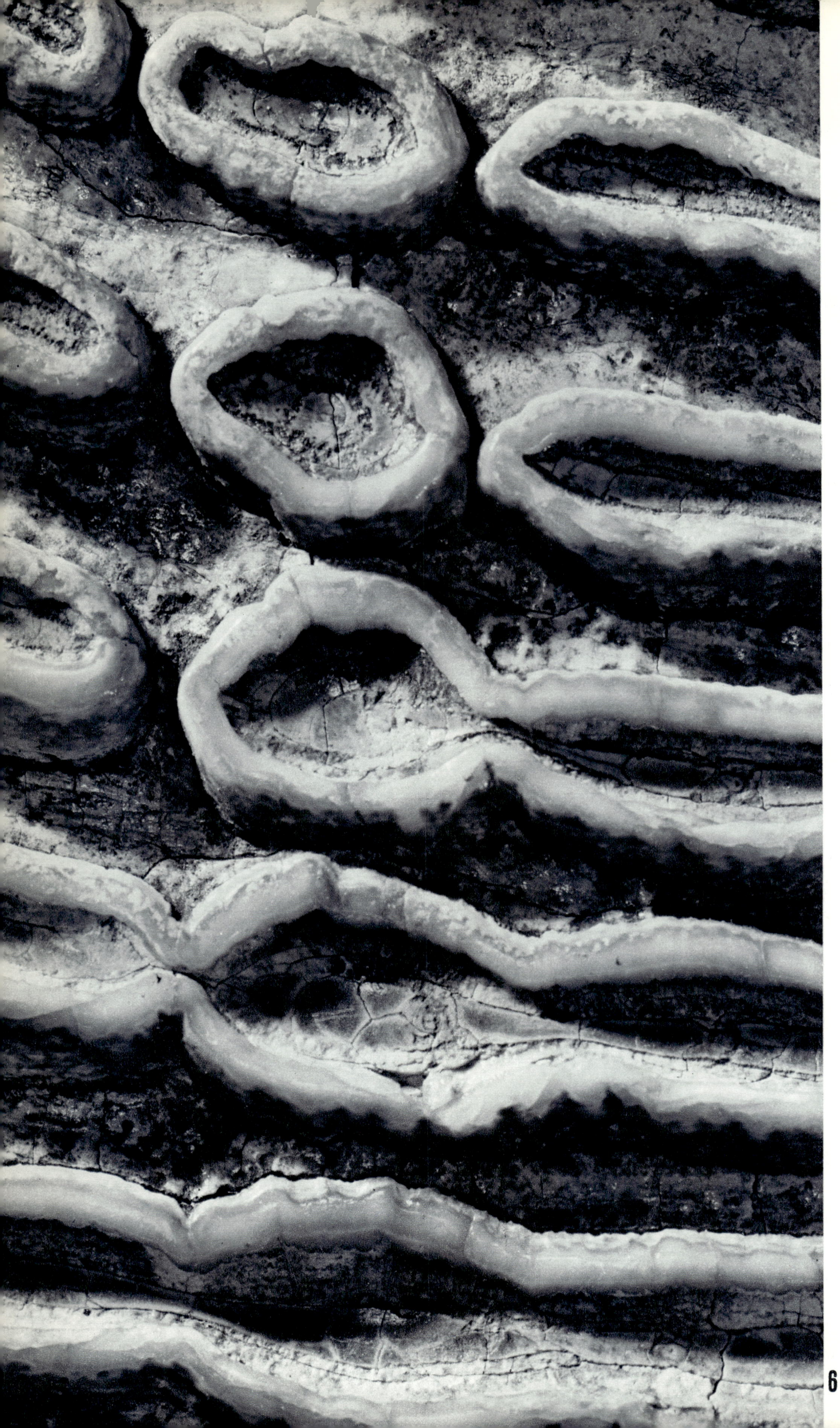

11

12

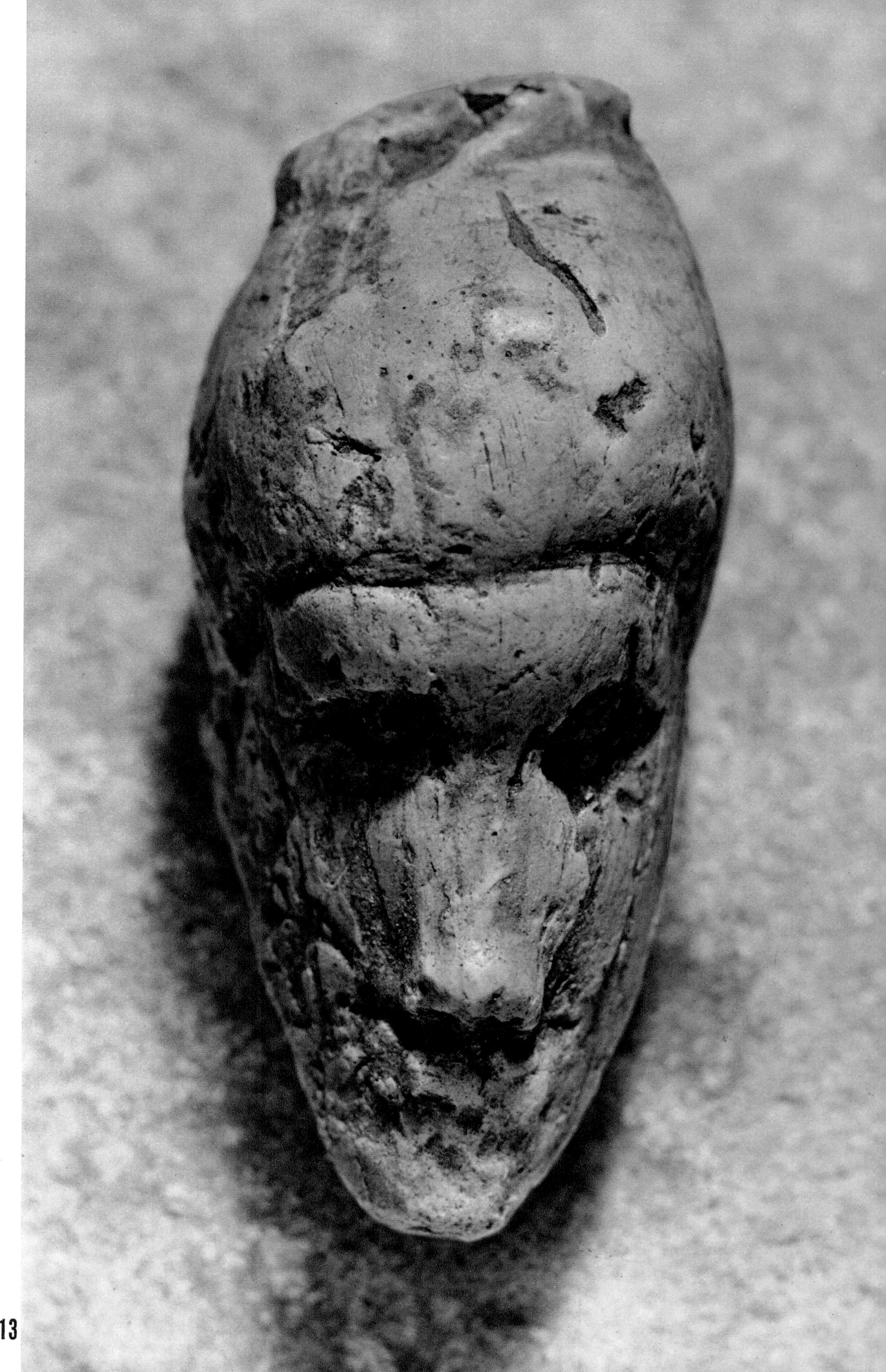

13

15

16

17

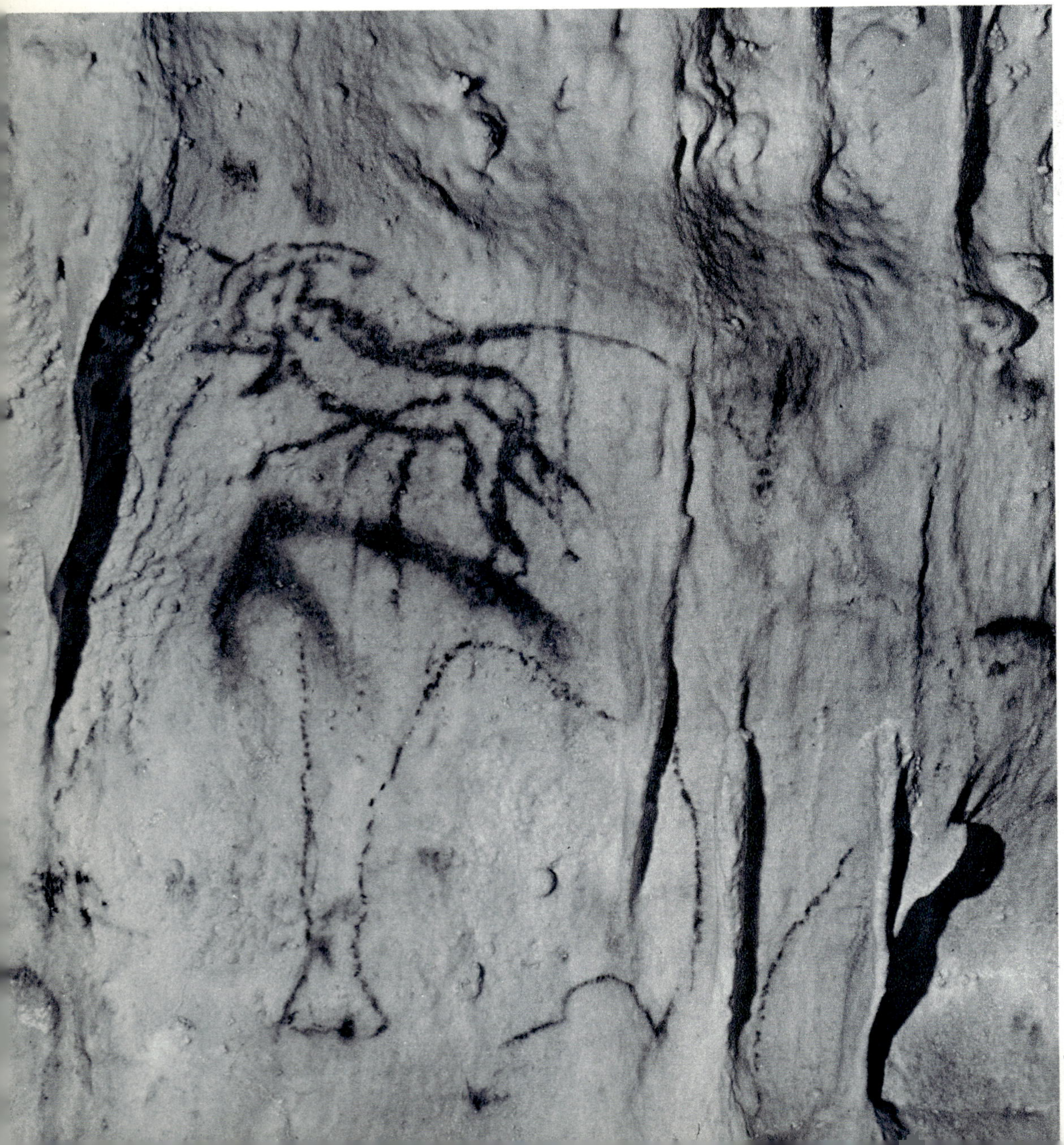

18

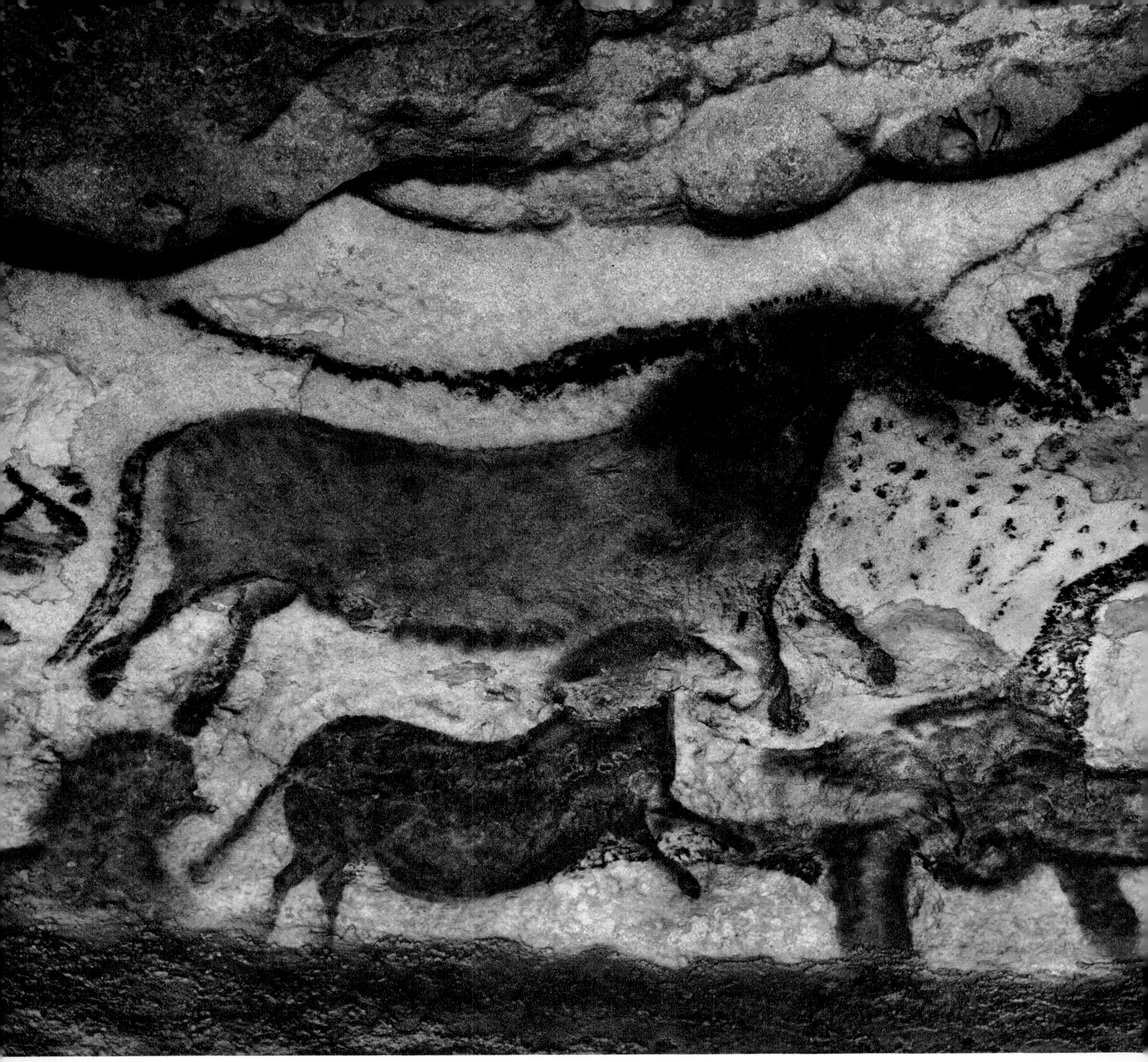

22

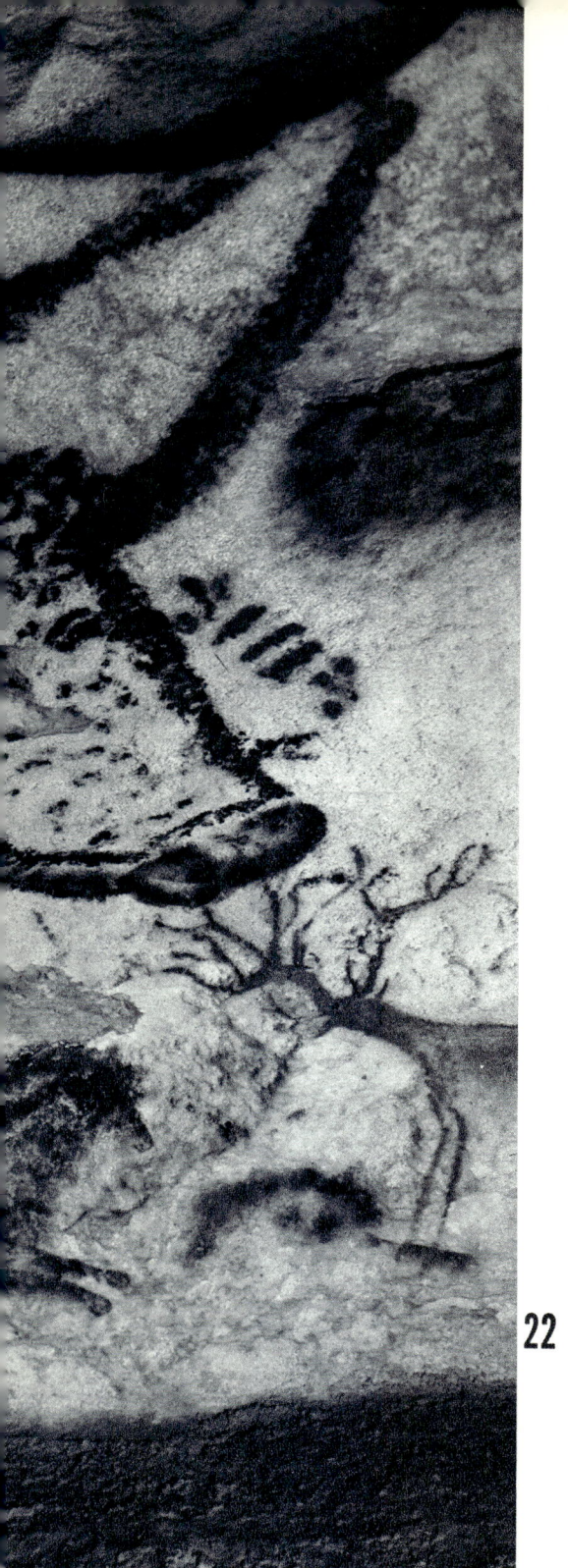

23

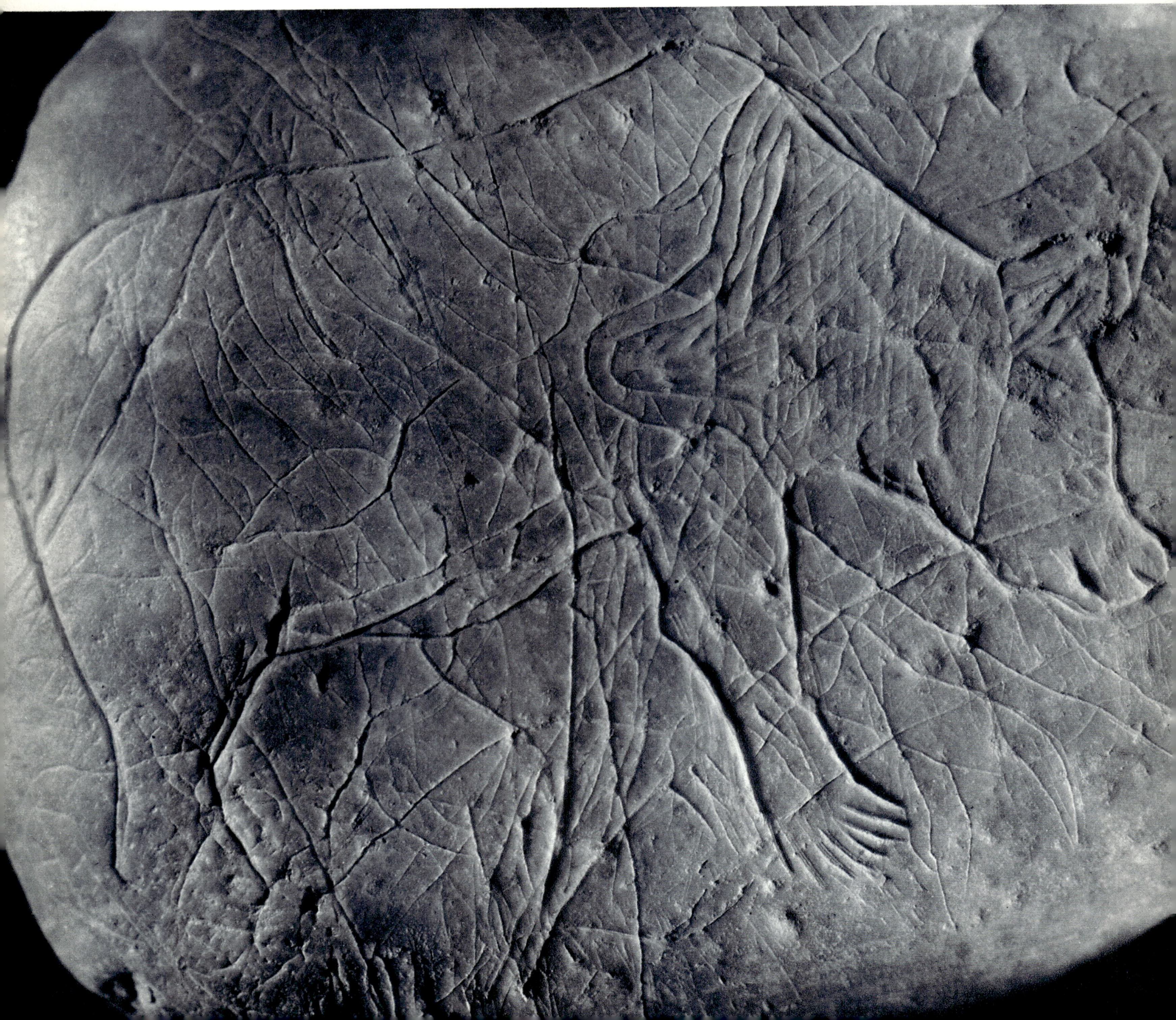

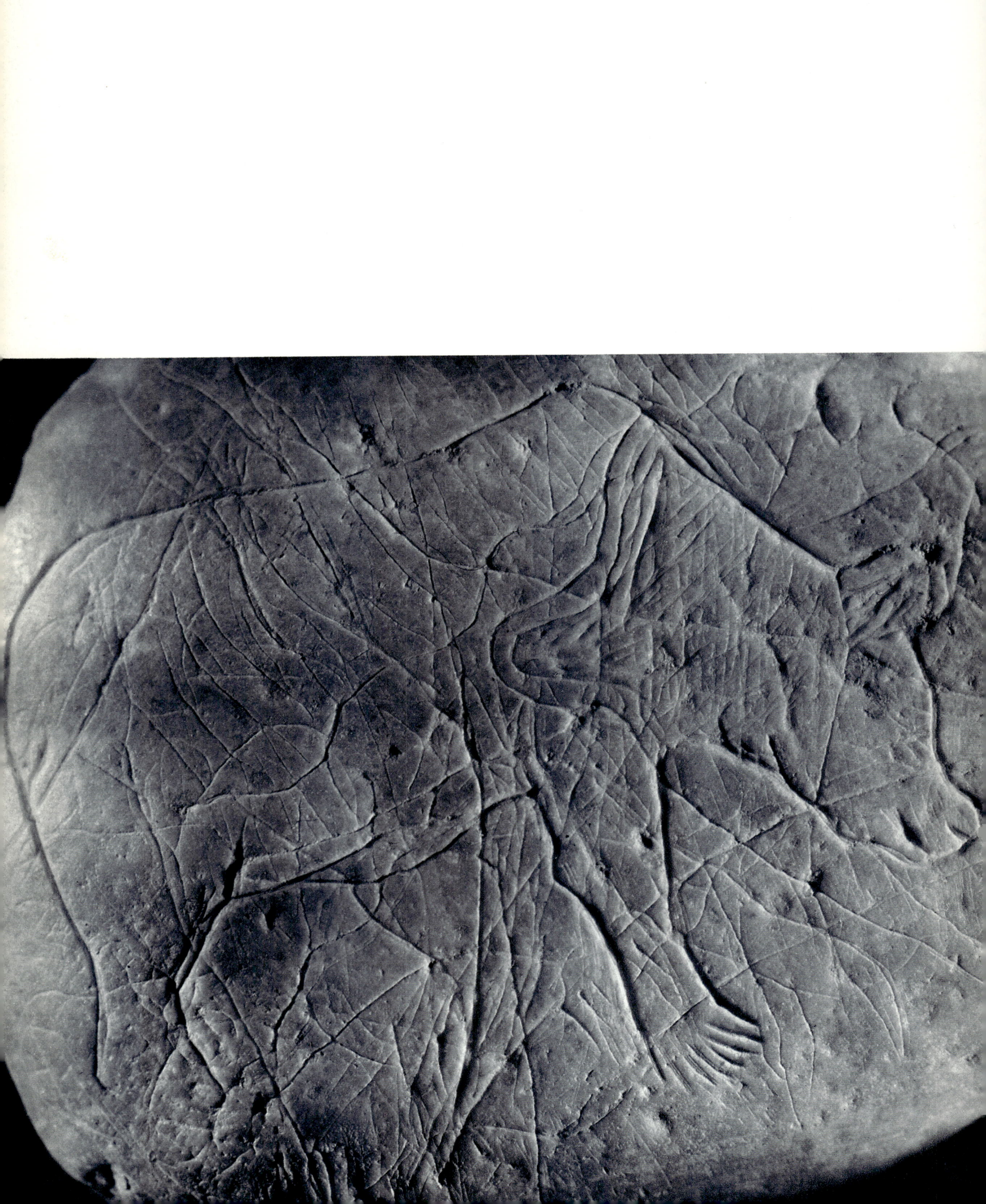

25

26

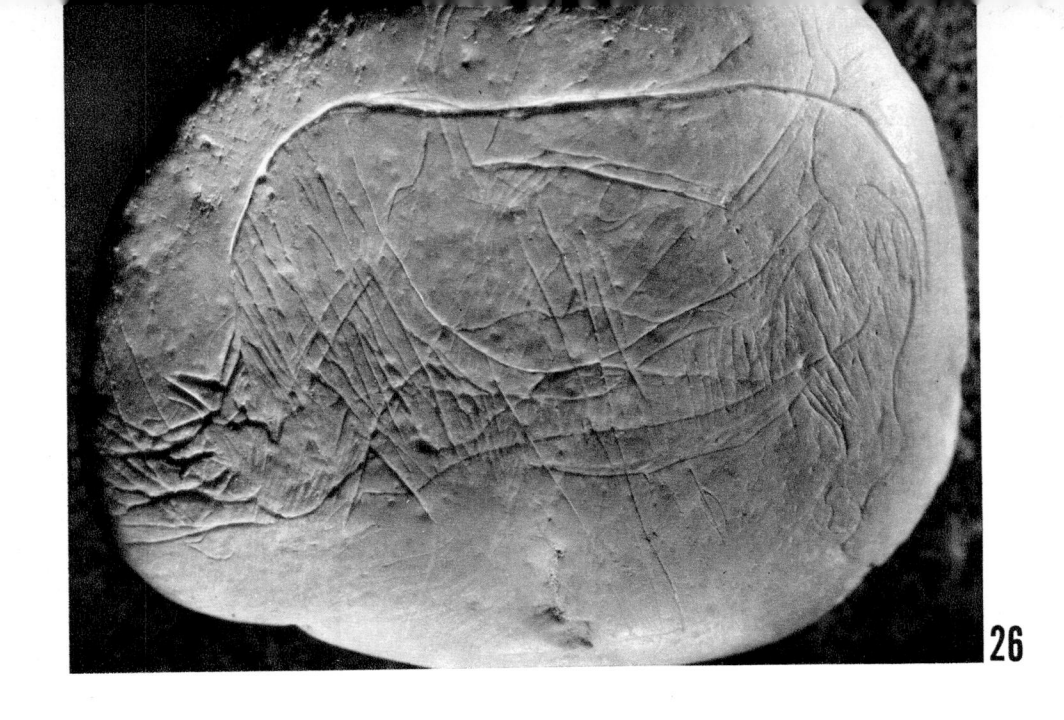

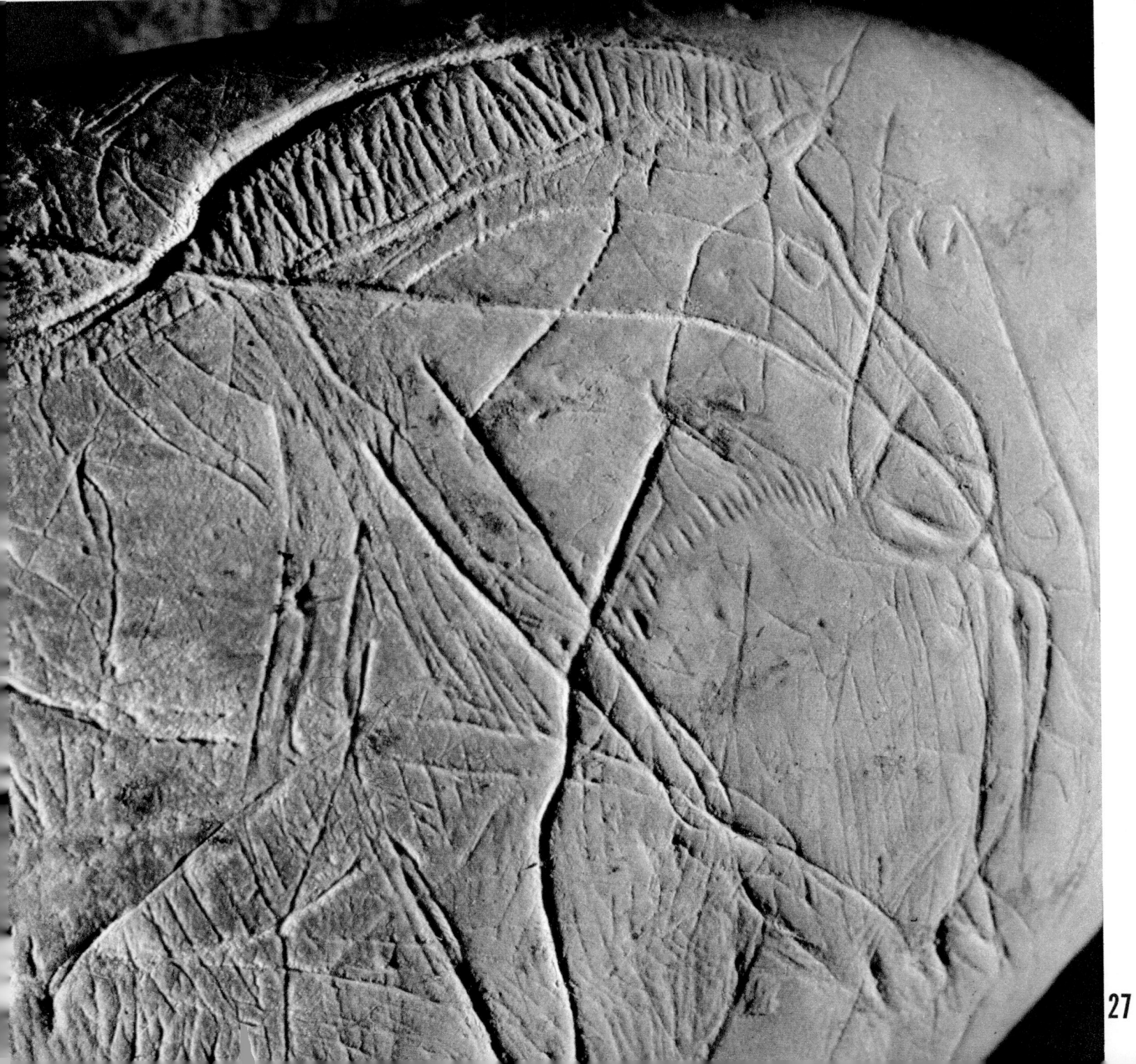

27

28

29

30

31

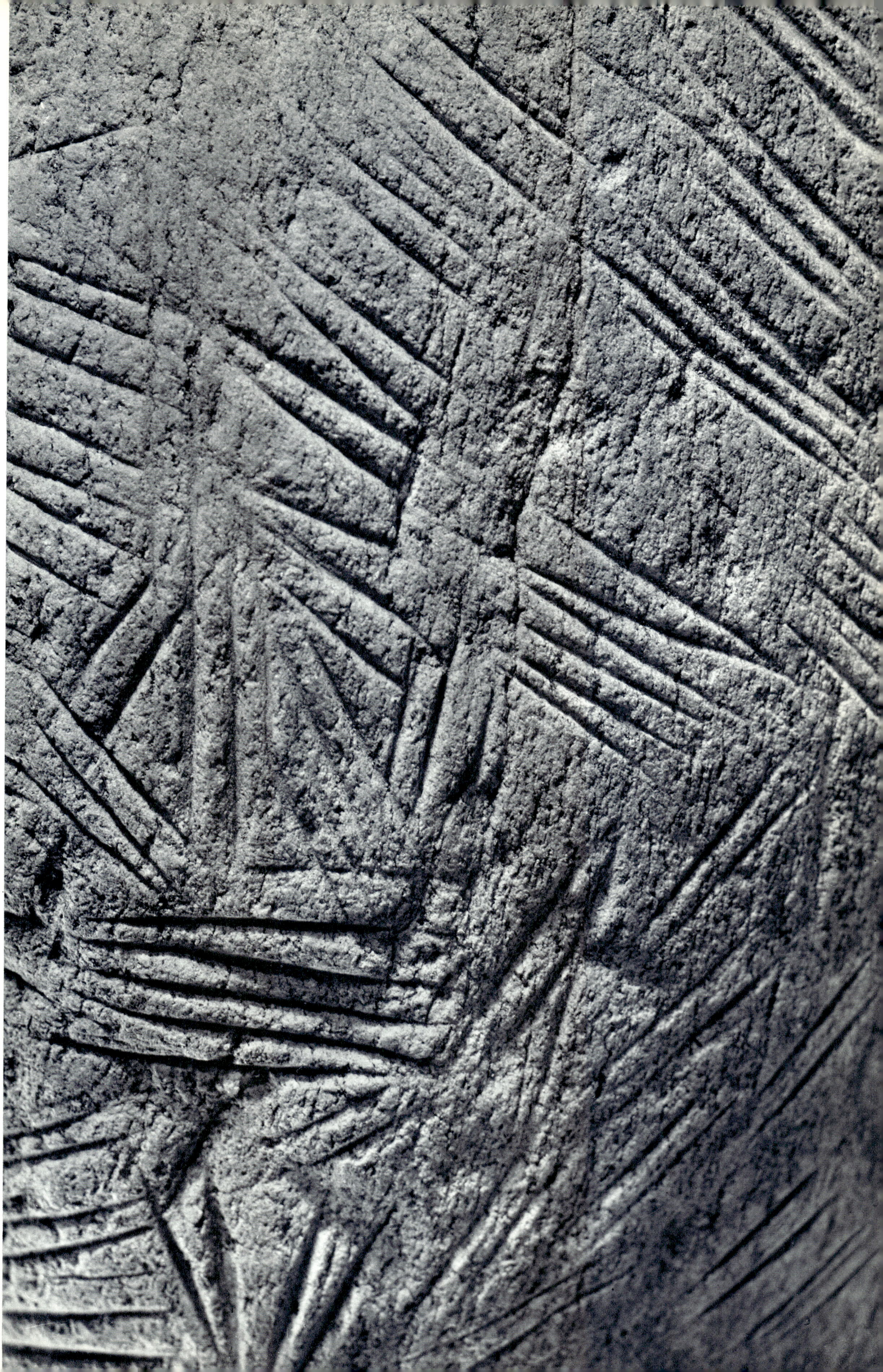

33

34

35

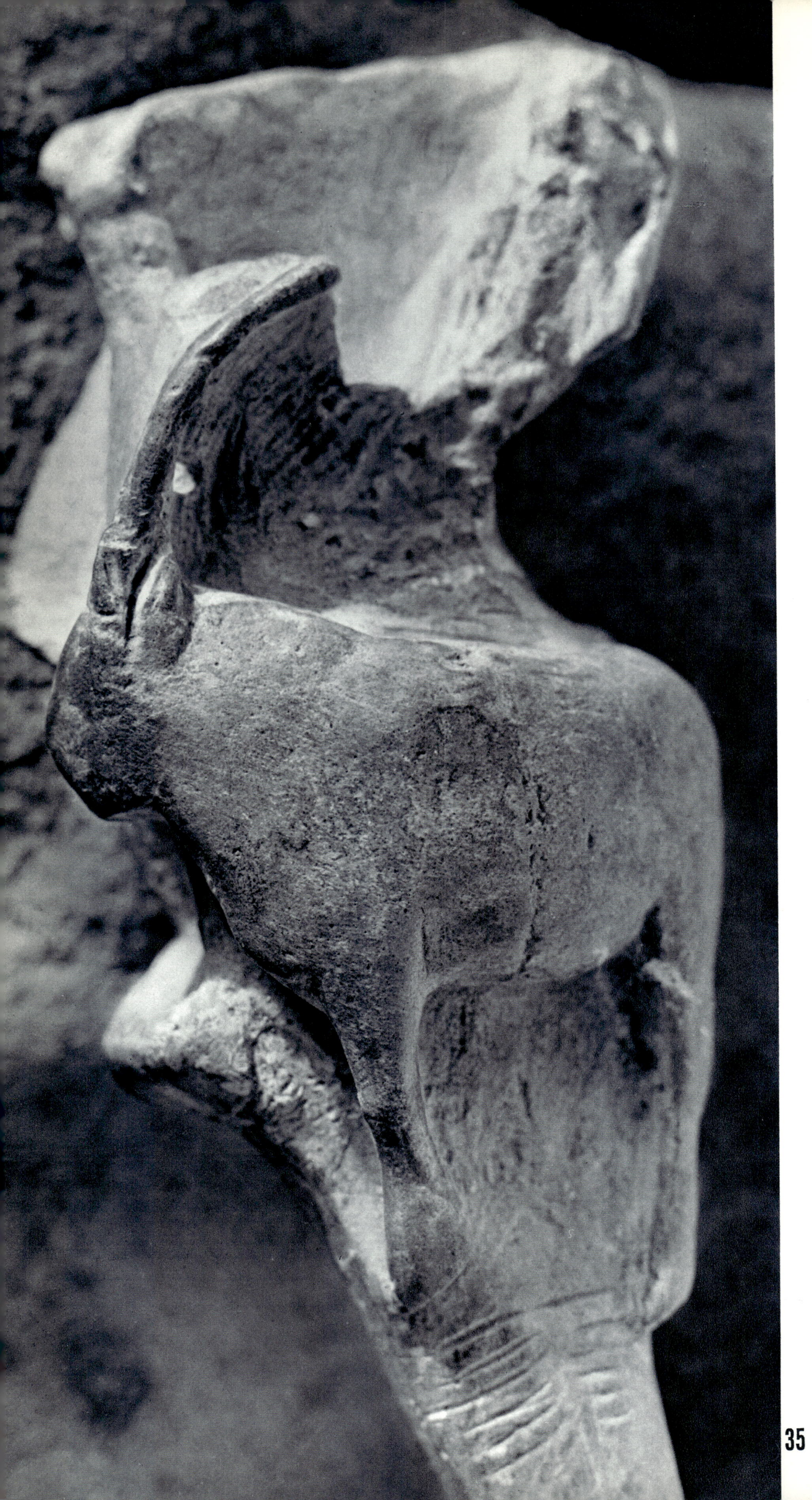

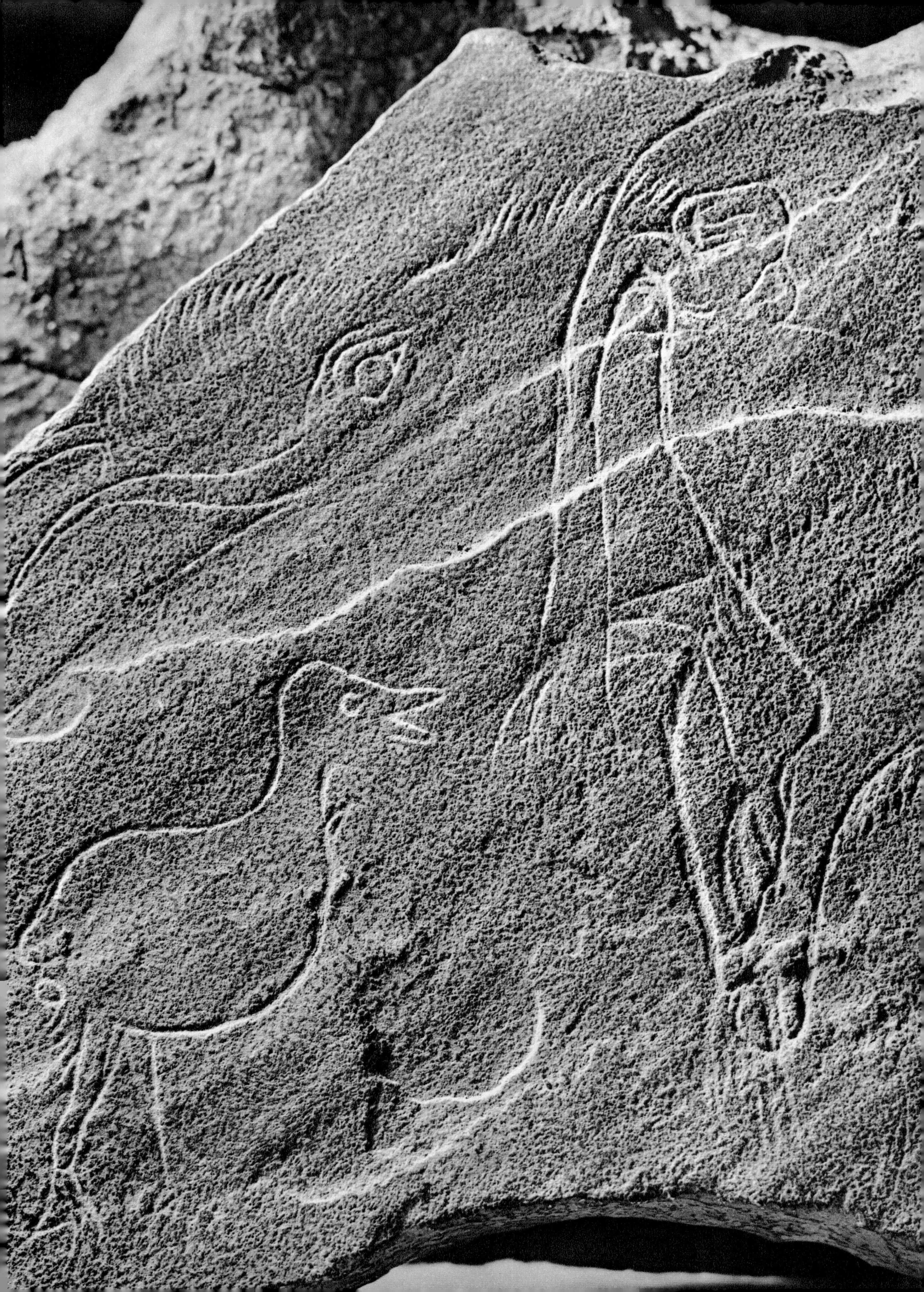

37

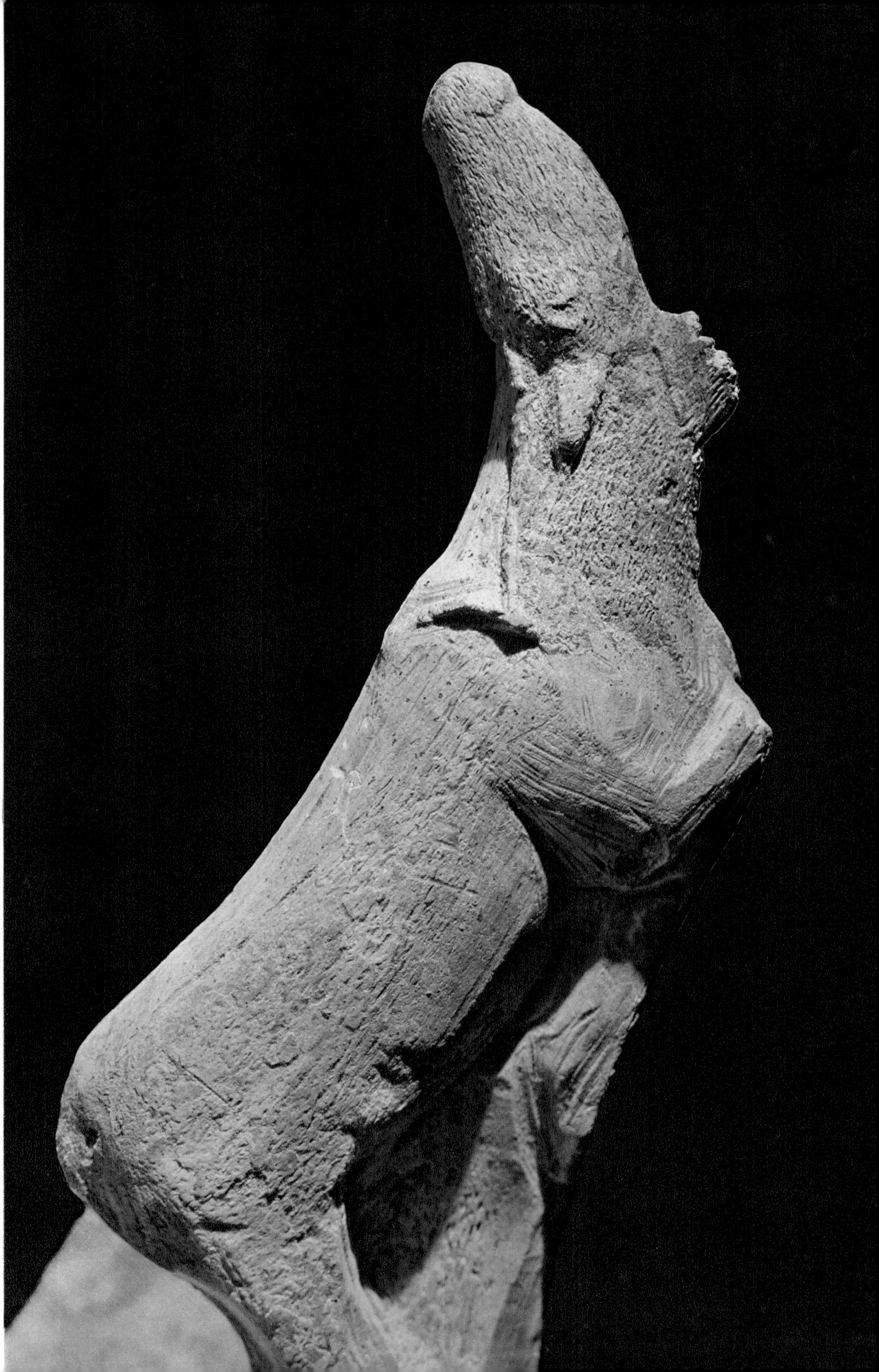

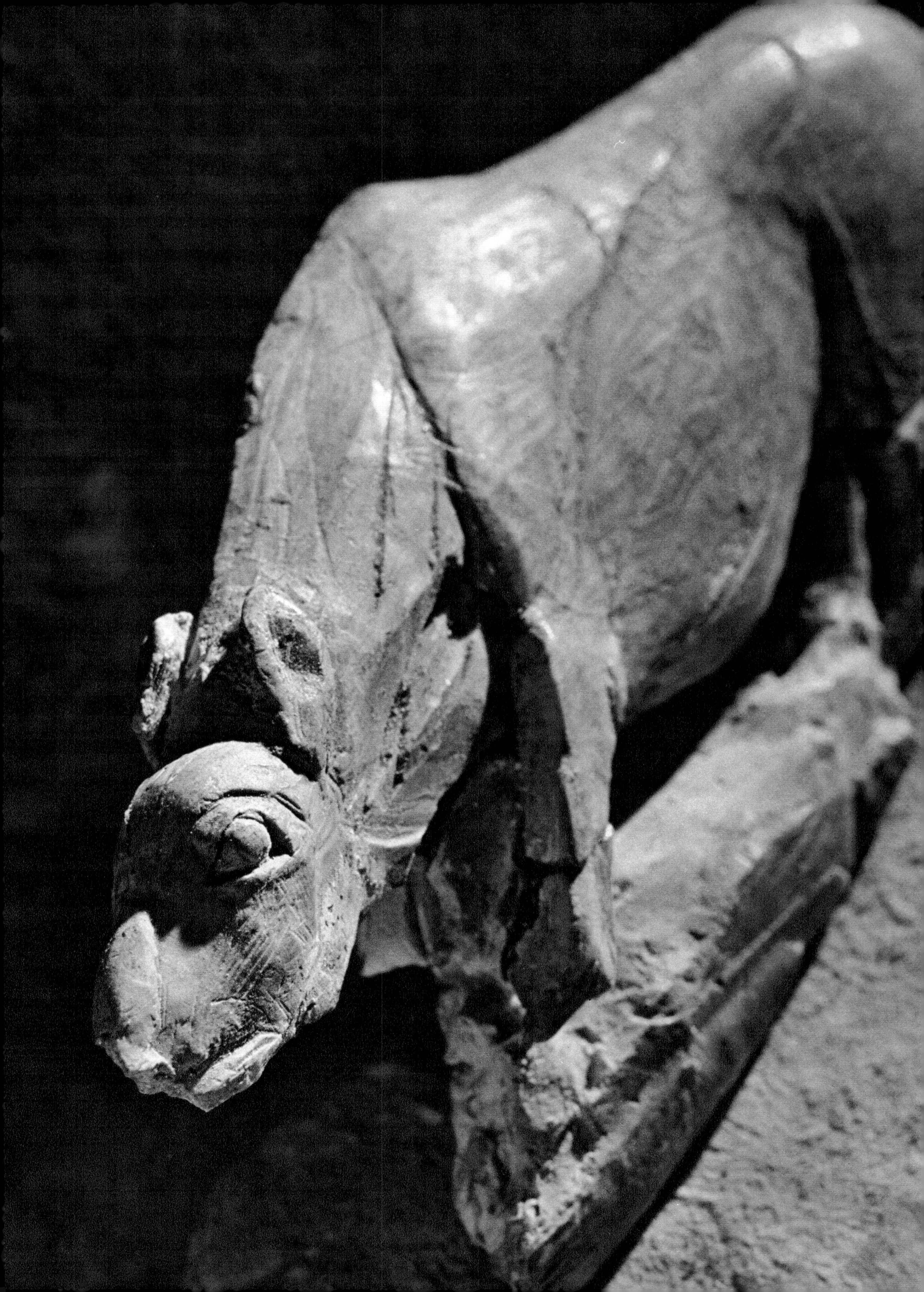

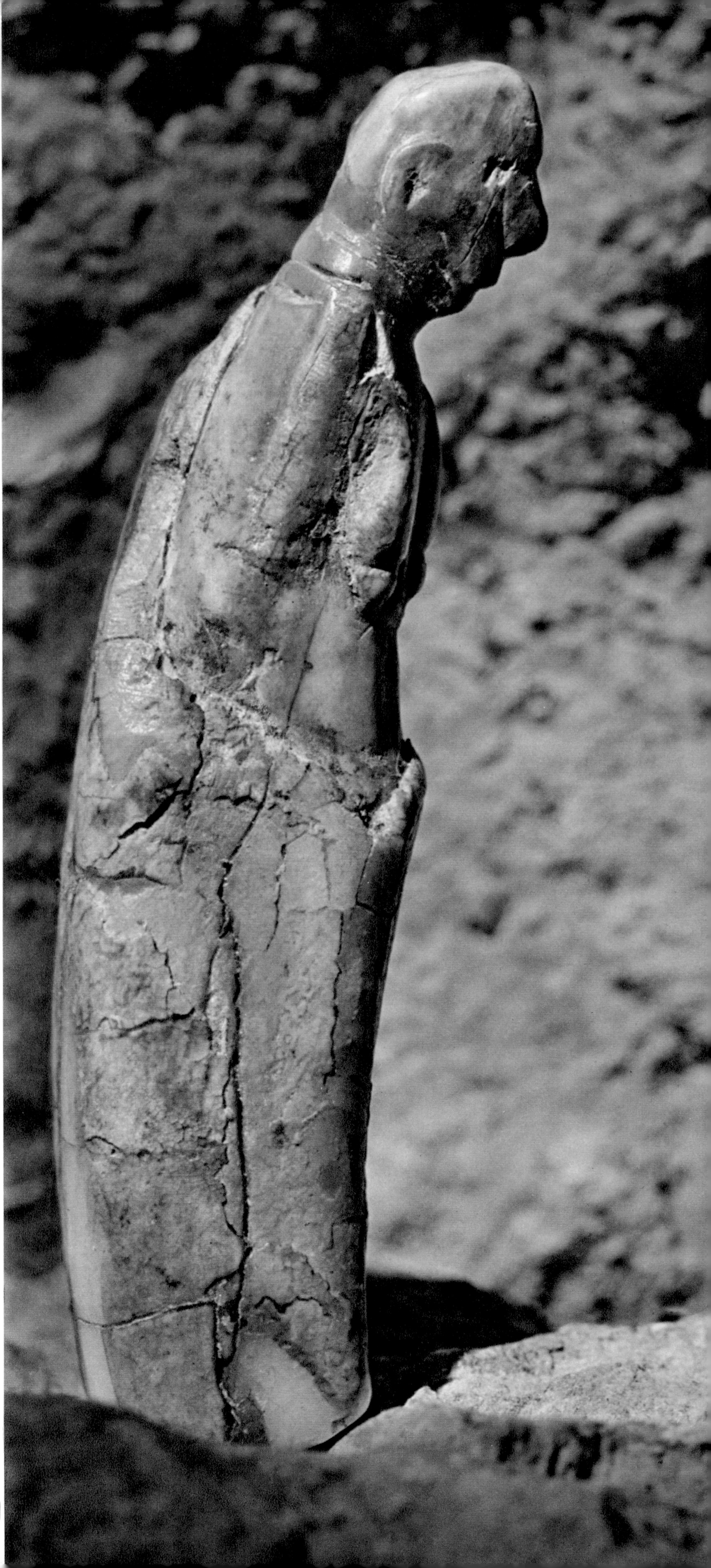

41

42

44

45

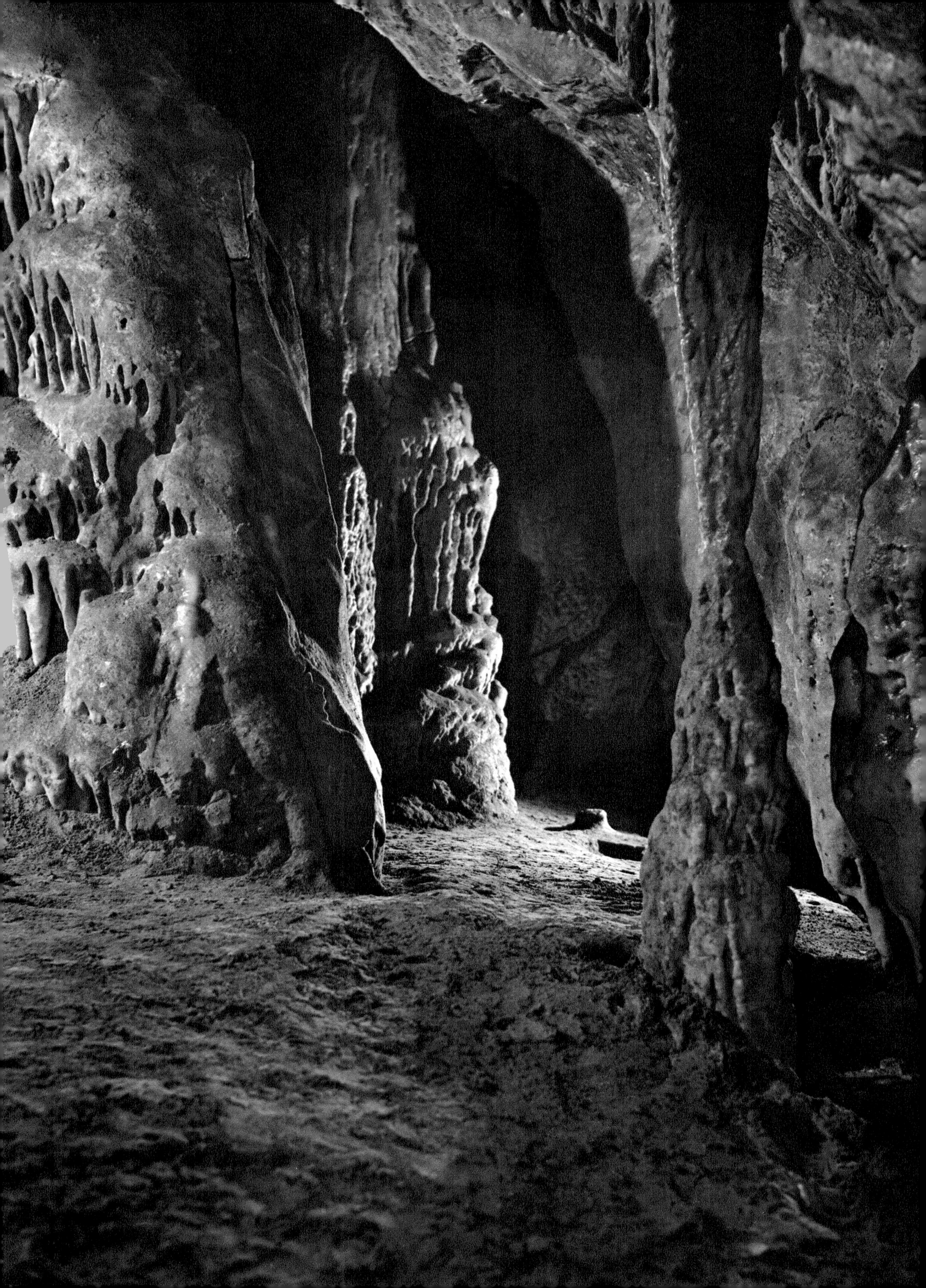

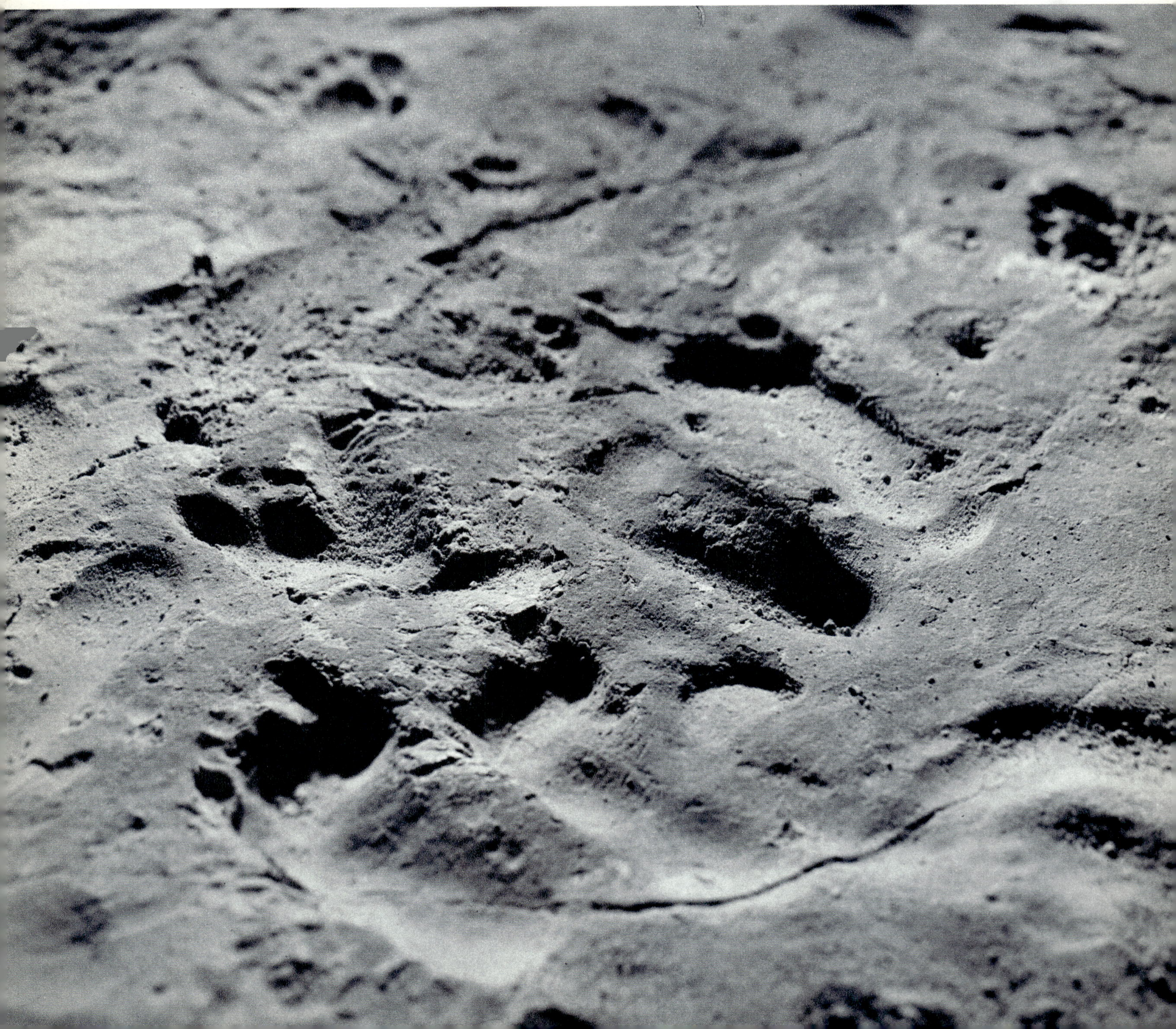

48

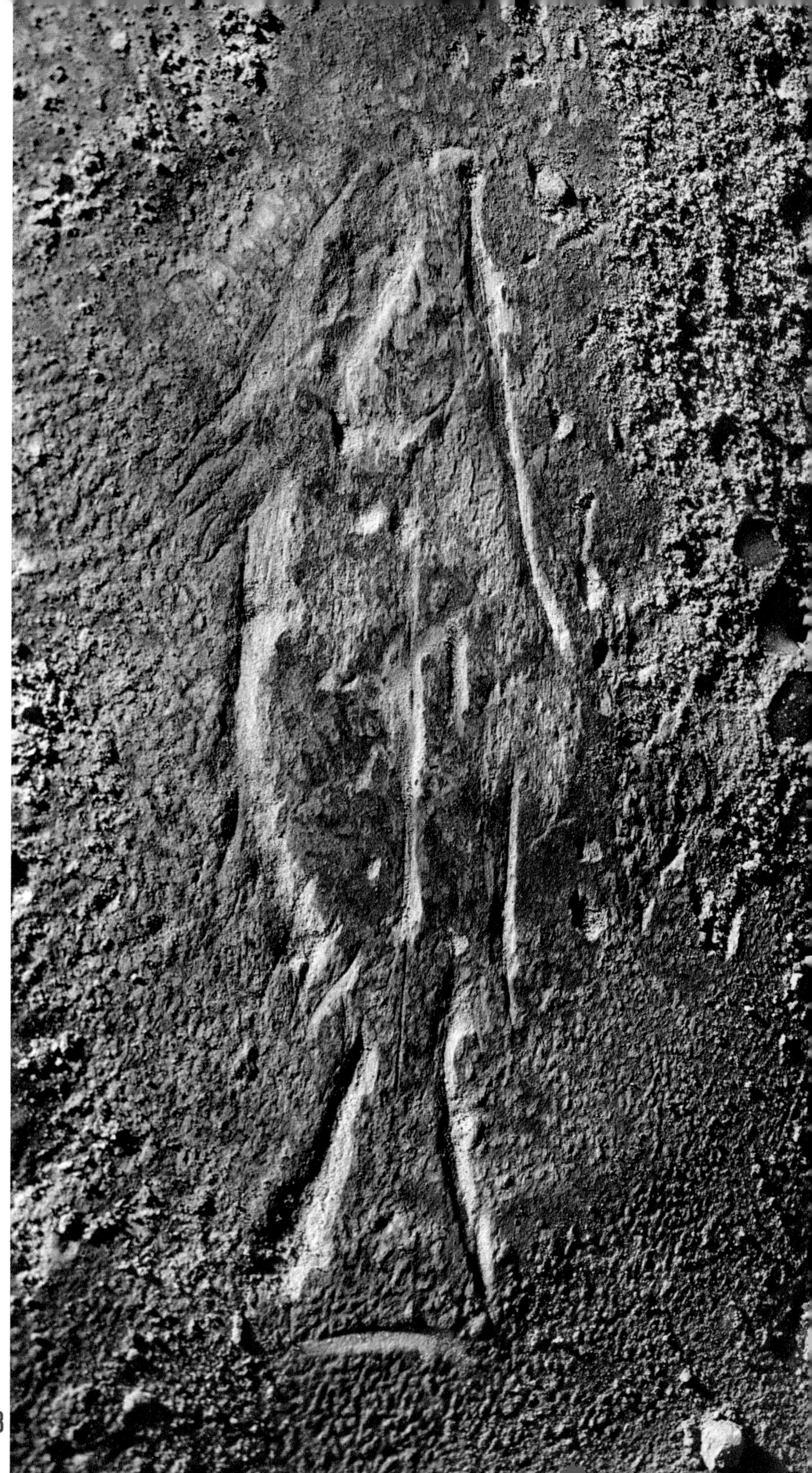

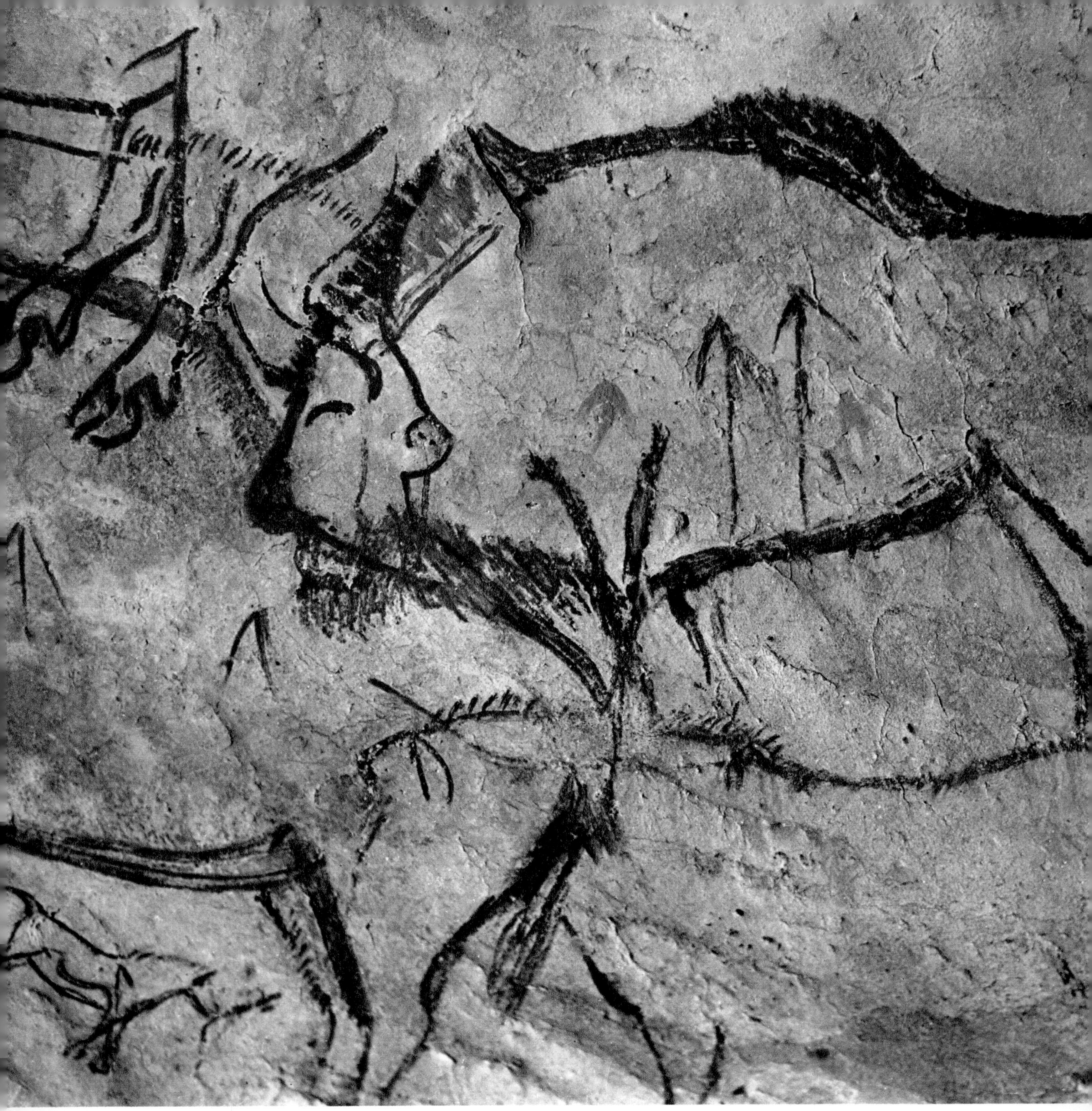

49

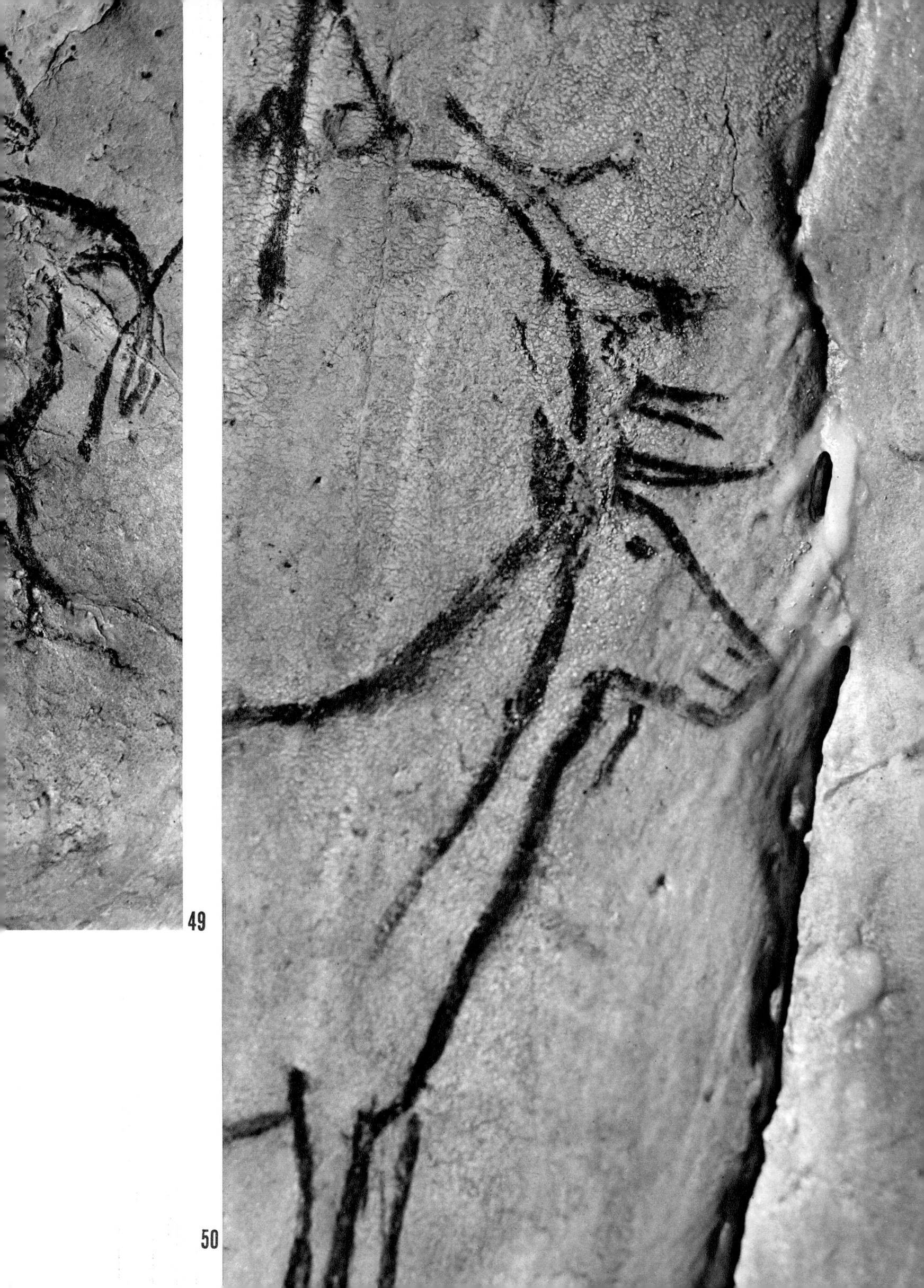

50

51

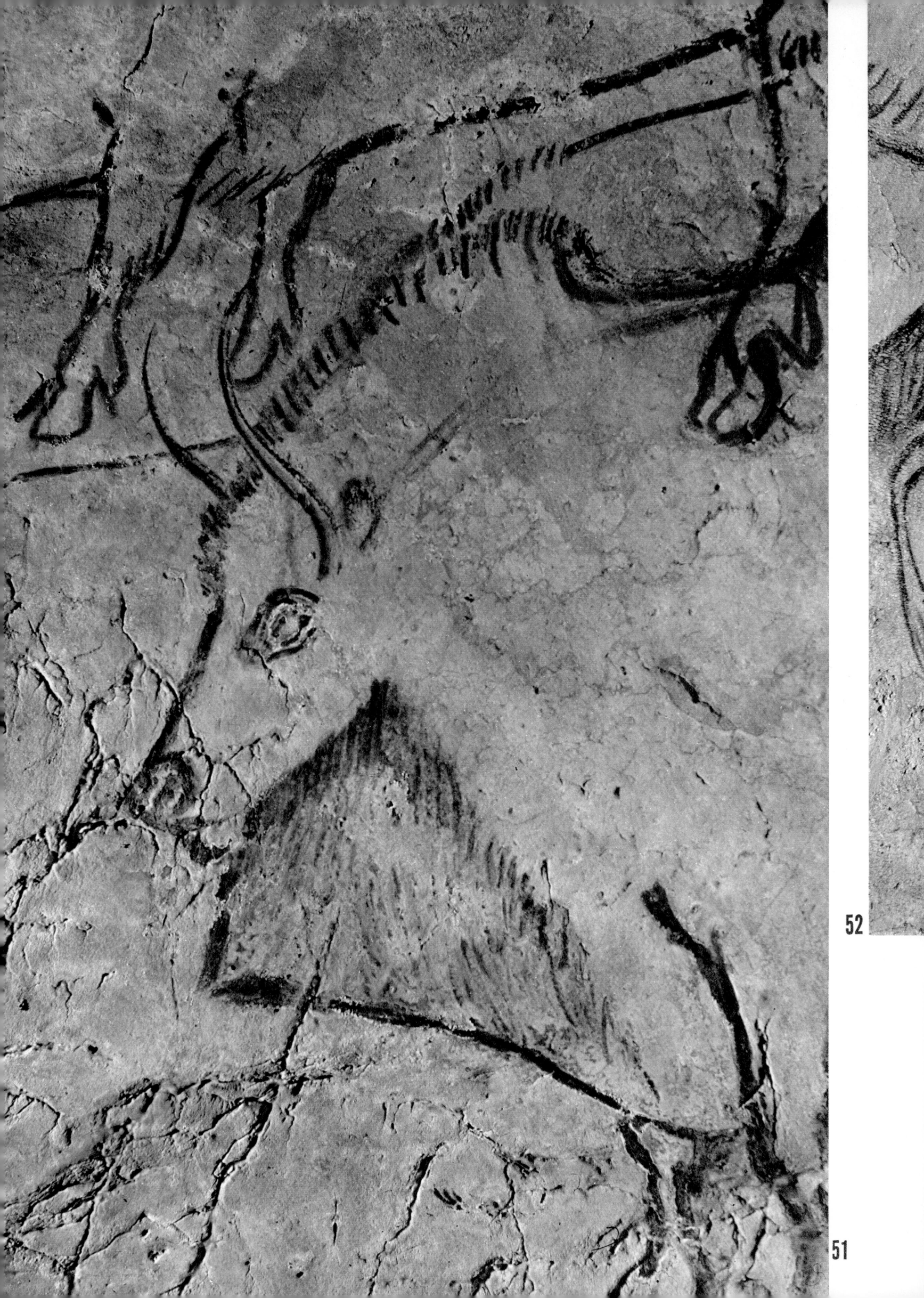

52

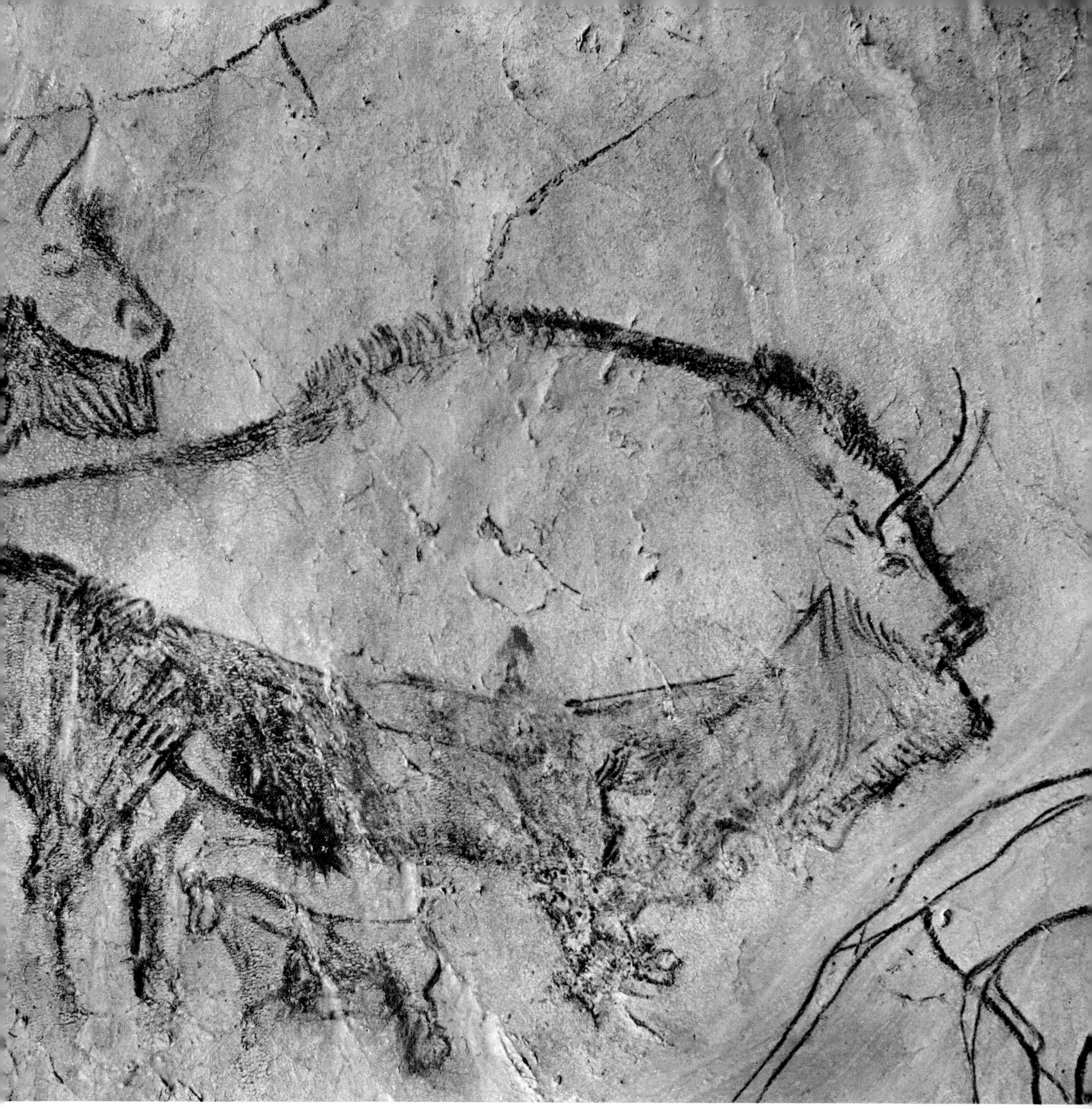

53

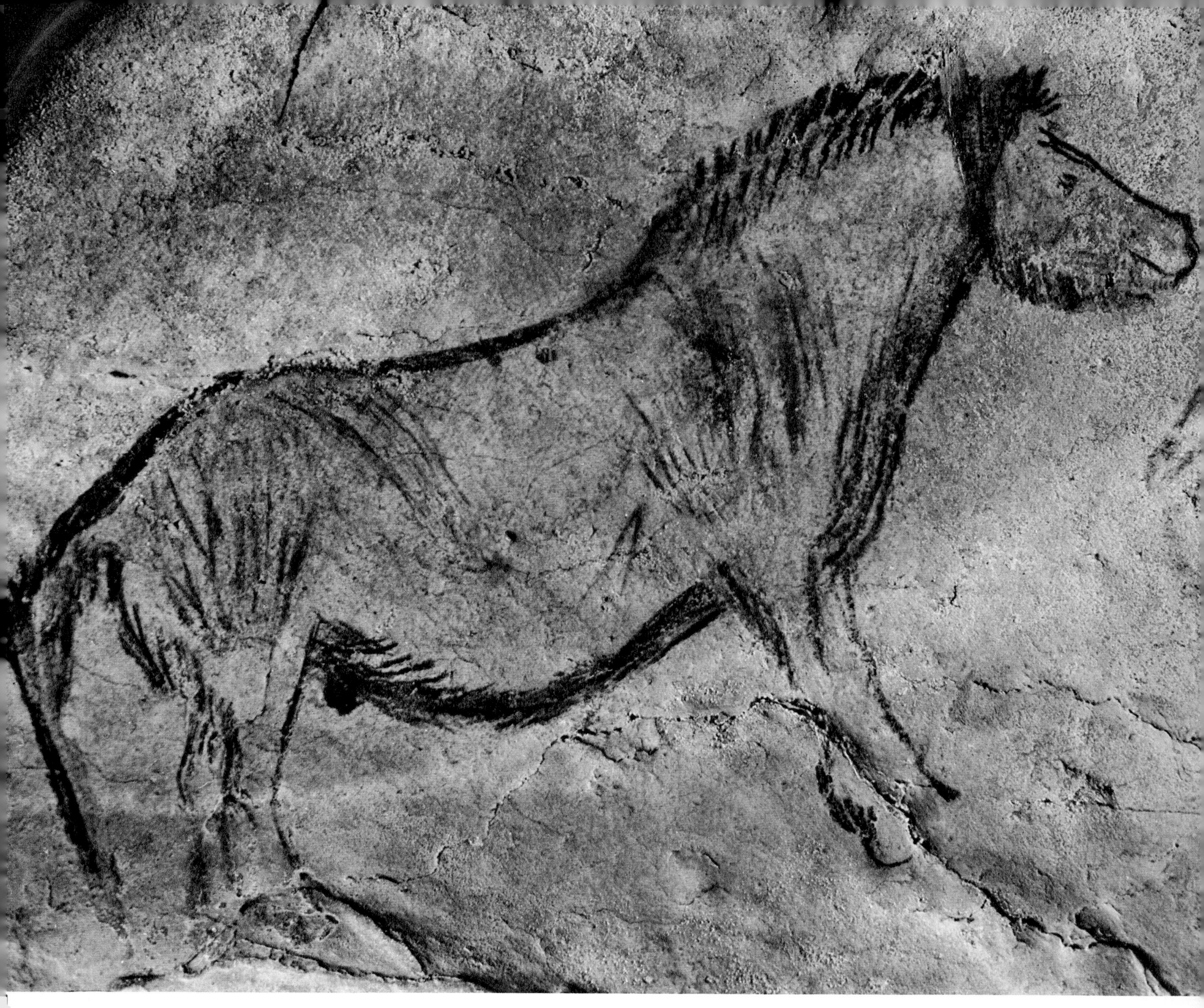

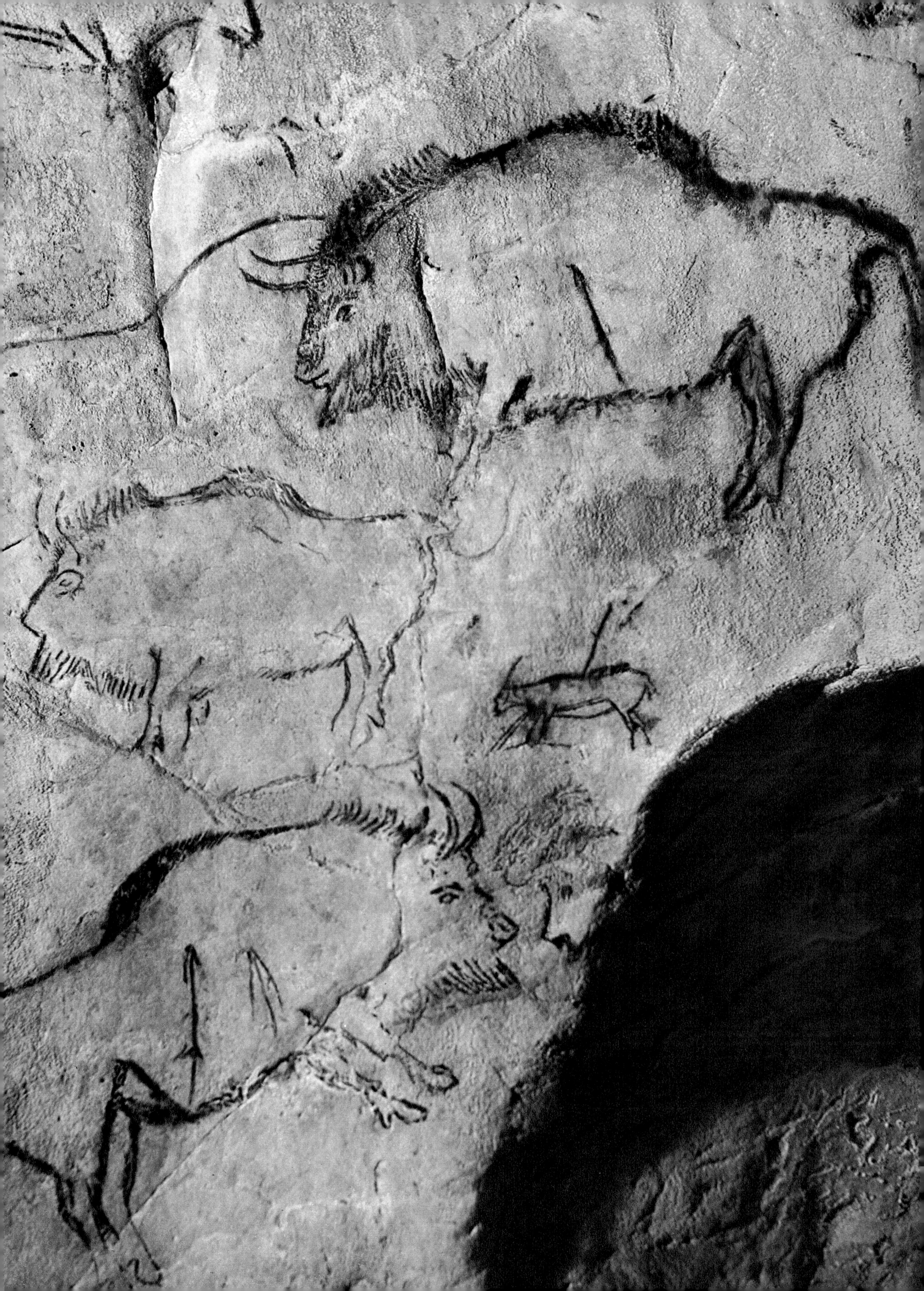

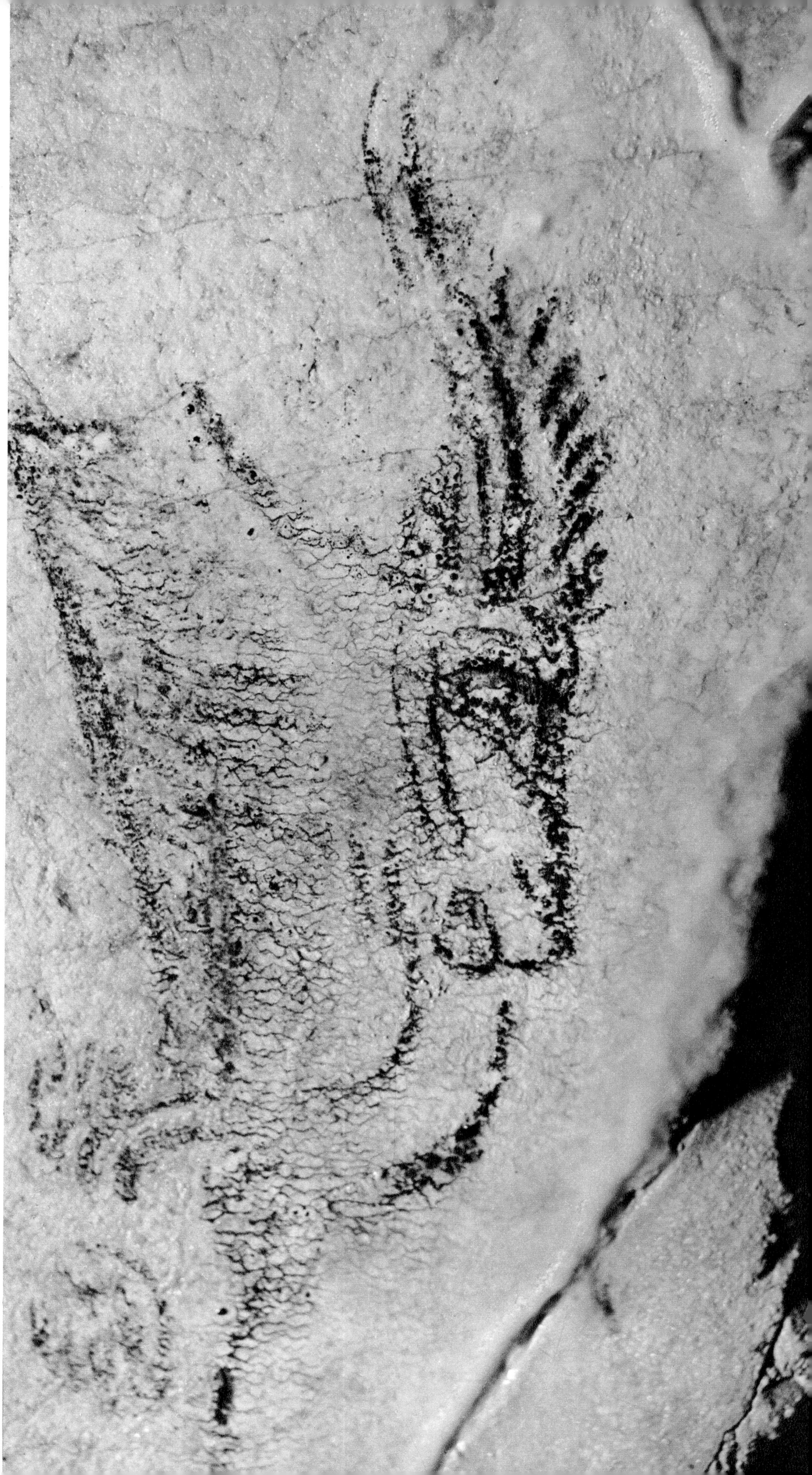

57

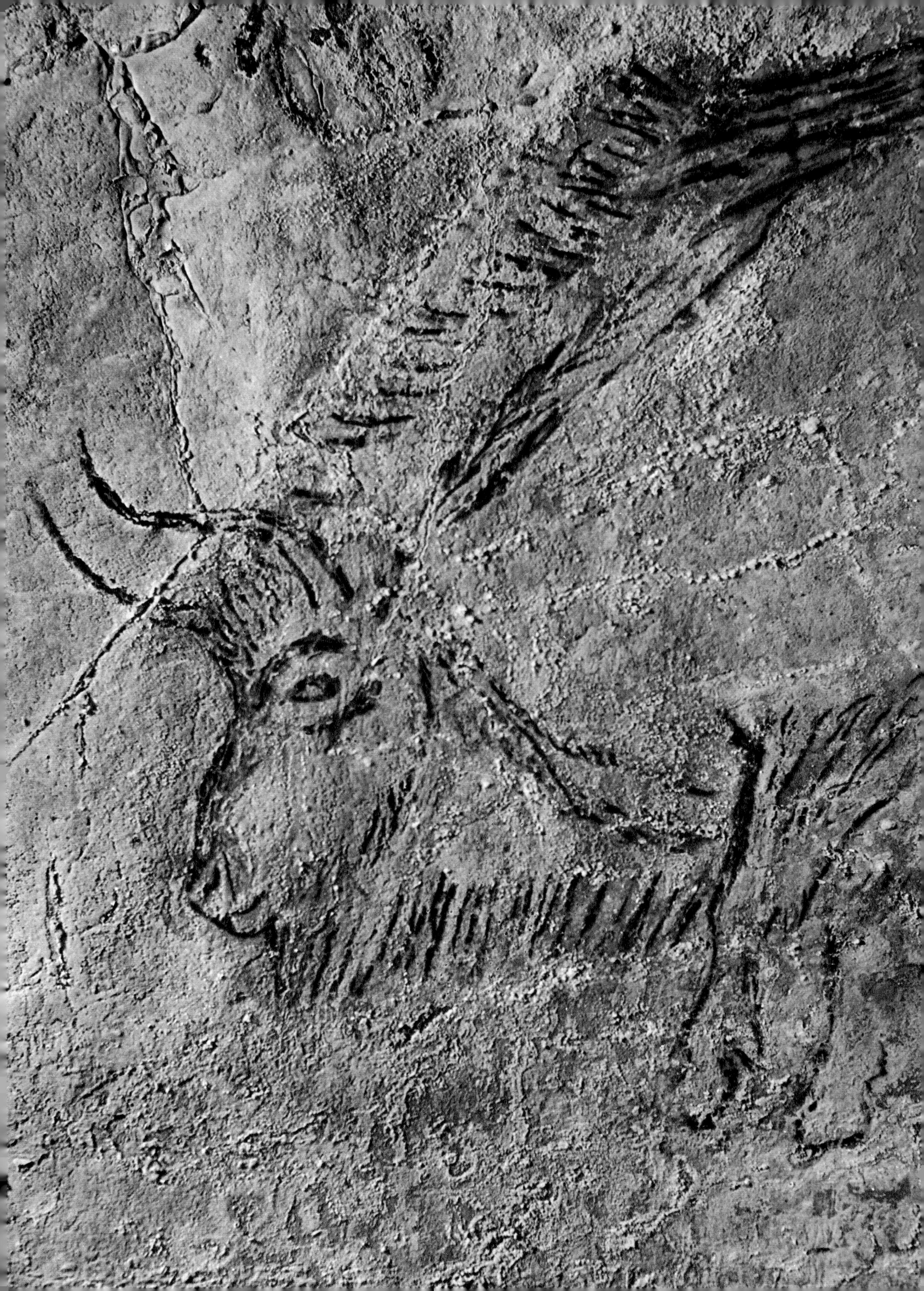

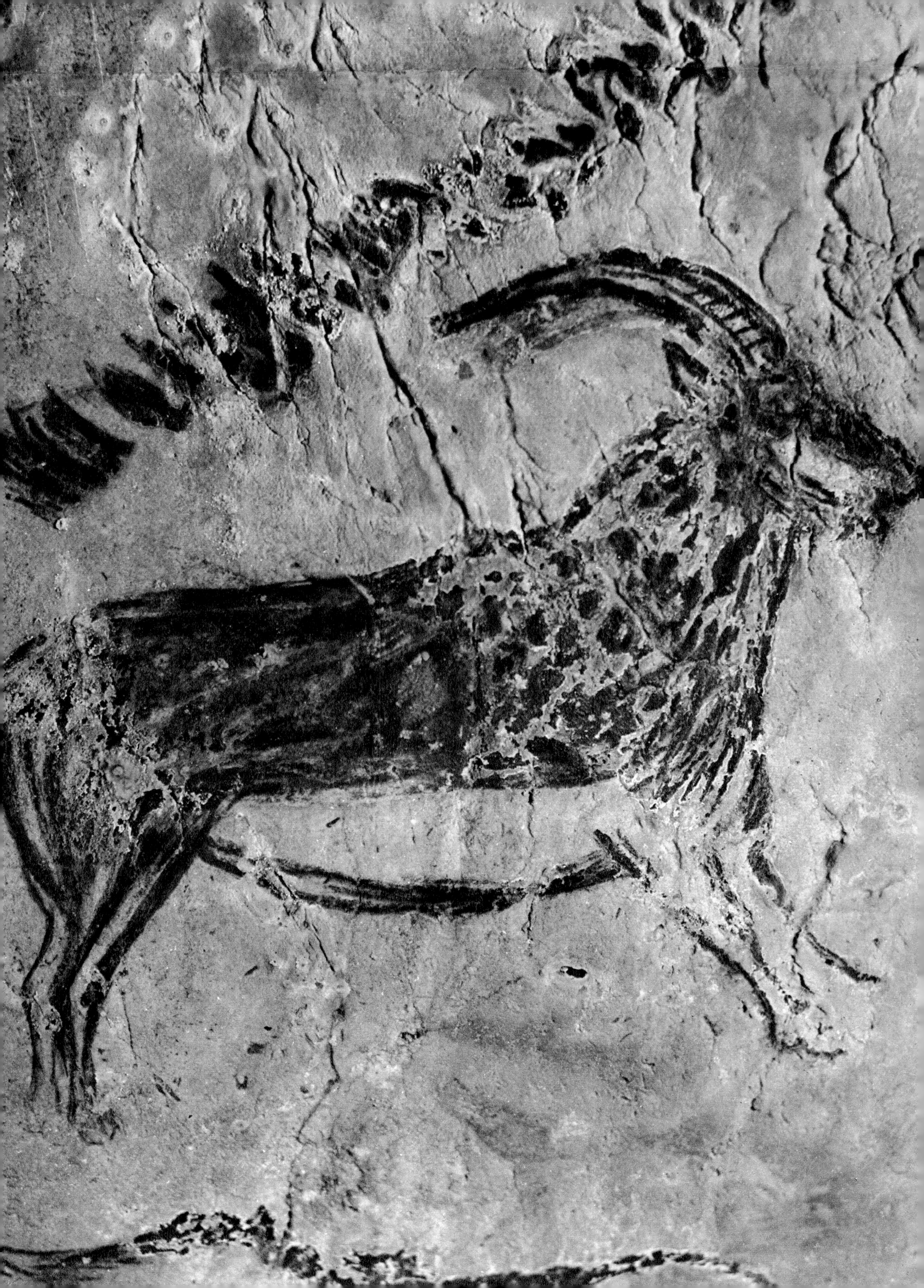

60

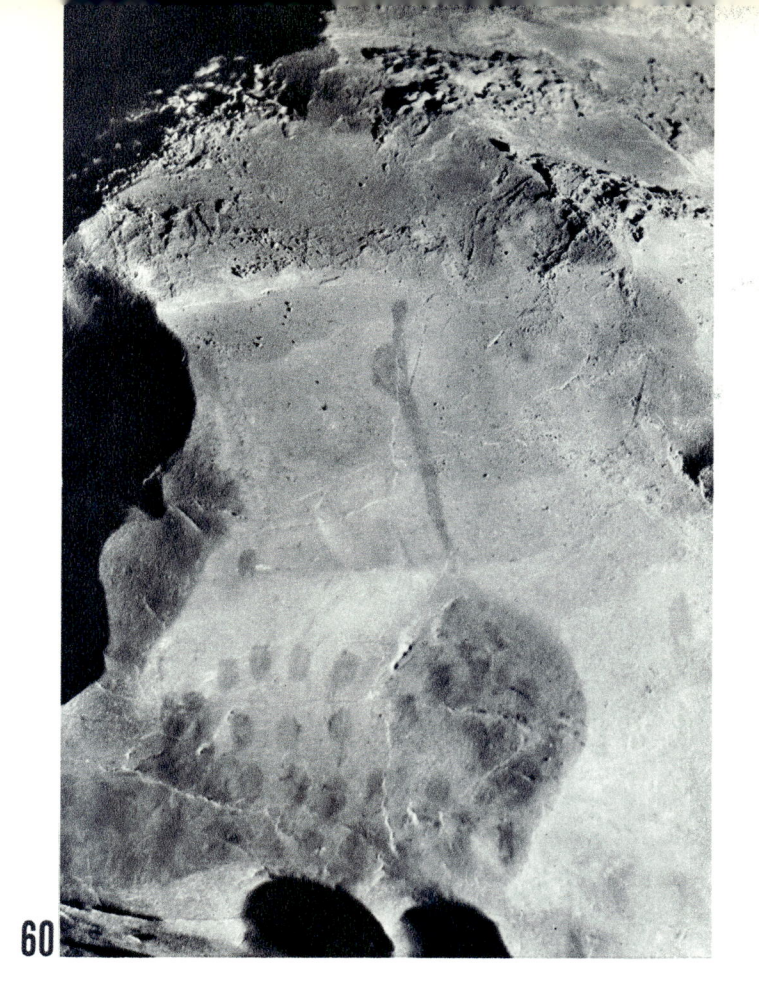

61

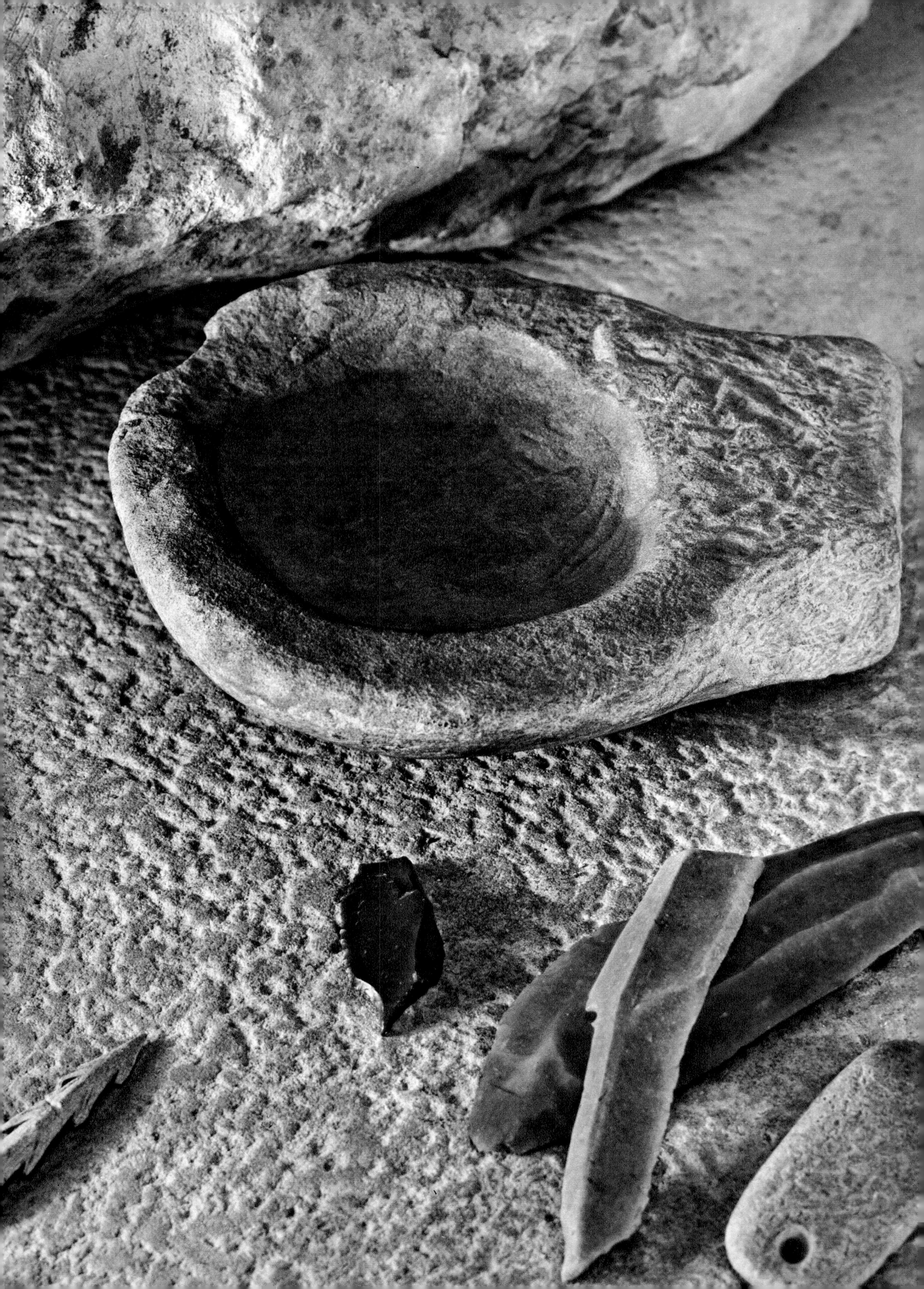

blows or rubs paint on to it; he removes his hand, the operation complete—and finds his hand shape stencilled on ground or rock by the colour.

He scrawls in the roof clay with his fingers, making the earliest primitive engravings. A finger sticky with a mixture of red ochre and fat from his body-painting leaves a red dab, a red line; and meander work turns to drawing with paint—to painting.

In the very magnificent cave of Pech-Merle, the images of which range through the early cycles of palæolithic art, there is a point where an ancient tumble of rocks stretches nearly up to the high ceiling, just where the ceiling is covered with glacial clay. Aurignacians scrambled up, and scrawled in that clay an ever-increasing mix-muddle of the images of their need. They scrawled images on the ceiling of mammoth, ibex, wild horse; they scrawled women, some headless, as if the body, the sheer fact of the matter, was all that concerned them, some, as it appears, with masked heads (compare the masked man and the headless man of Cougnac in Plates 18 and 16), but all of them gravid, with full bellies and heavy swinging breasts; and elsewhere in Pech-Merle, on the clay, appears a scrawl-drawing made with the tip of the finger of that *Cervus megaceros* depicted in red line in Cougnac.

In addition to the scrawl-drawings, and later drawings of the range of the huntsman's fauna, Pech-Merle as well displays its startling hands silhouetted with red or black, particularly upon a vertical slab of limestone standing up from the floor, around spotted paintings of two life-sized wild horses.

Scrawl-drawings with the finger are abandoned for drawings with the tool which is an extension of the finger, which is, so to say, the finger drawn out to a finer point,—whether that tool is the bone or stick or flint engraver or the brush which carries the pigment. Slowly bettering and refining his skill, gaining in grace and freedom and firmness, the Aurignacian in early phases of palæolithic art shows himself at times no inconsiderable draughtsman. Indeed Aurignacians may have been the first artists of the great colour-cave of Lascaux (though the Lascaux images of Plates 22 and 23 spring from a later vision).

But sculpture? Where, so far as they can be discerned or suggested, does sculpture have its beginnings? Where again, and when, in this increasing light or this stædy amelioration of the estate of man?

If man becomes adept at releasing the foreseen image of a tool from flint or bone or wood, it would seem a transition very simple and obvious from releasing tool-images to releasing from the raw natural stuff an image of man or game. In fact, though, we are more lazy and conservative than it is fashionable to allow. Man does what he cannot escape doing without much willingness as a rule, and without much enthusiasm. If he changes, he is inclined to do so by jump or by imitation: he will imitate the energy and inventions of clever individuals or take over some innovation, as it is to him, from newcomers in his territory. The lazy answer—or question—is, Why carve in stone, if that hasn't become your habit in ritual and magical affairs, when more expeditiously and with far less trouble you can go on drawing, engraving, and painting?

Our arts, primitive or sophisticated, are much conditioned by convenience, and by availability of material. In South Africa, Bushman painting developed where caves and shelters provided the right sheltered rocky surfaces. In the high veldt of the interior, without caves and shelters, engraving was the rule. In Australia, arid regions without shelters or caves have an art only of portable objects; whereas in Northern Kimberley and Arnhem Land circumstances all in unison—plenty of caves and shelters, plenty of food, not too much moving about from place to place, and so plenty of time—have promoted a rich cavern art of painted images. Or come to Europe again: in modern France, modern England, we have long had sculptors as well as painters: stone is available. In Holland of dykes and dunes stone is not available, so painters alone, and not sculptors, are the Dutch cultural product.

In palæolithic France the two-dimensional pictorial complex was favoured—once it had rooted itself—both by man's laziness and by conditions. Life was not too mobile, there was food, by early standards population was fairly dense. Materials were at hand for engraving-tools, in the limestone red ochre was plentiful, smooth sheets of limestone in cave after cave offered clean " canvases " and clean " plates ".

In the Gravettian, or East Gravettian, culture of the steppes of Russia, south of the ice, and in Eastern Europe, it was a different matter. Men had to move to live. Nomad hunters followed mammoth and rhino and other quarry across the cold plains. They were *Homo sapiens* with the neat skull, but their different culture was adapted to altogether different conditions and to a climate pitiless and still colder—at least in winter. Lacking the *abris*, lacking the comfort of the deep limestone gorges of the Dordogne and the Lot and their tributaries, and of the limestone hills of Pyrenean France and Spain between the Picos de Europa and the Bay of Biscay, these Gravettian hunters built huts against the blizzard, digging them partly into the ground and using mammoth bones as walling. The wind howled, the temperature dropped: in the snowy winter world of the steppes these Gravettians even made use of coal, where it outcropped, for their fires.

No less than Aurignacians, the Gravettians of the East had a stake in the fertility of wives and food-animals; but their limited and peculiar economy inclined them to carving and modelling rather than to painting. Mammoths, above all, gave these incessant nomads food and materials; including materials for art. Since they were nomads, their desire images had to be light and portable and small; so they carved little figurines from mammoth ivory. They developed, in their little " Venuses " or mother-goddesses, which have occurred from Austria and Czechoslovakia to Siberia, an art of formal relationships and symbolic simplifications which was exceedingly expert. As well as ivory from the great curving tusks of the mammoth, they also used for their figurines a kind of terracotta of clay and burnt mammoth bone, though it might be going a little far to call them the first potters of the world.

To see one of the famous figurines in a glass case in a museum is something of a surprise. In photographs they are monumental: in fact, great figures which looked from the photograph as if they might have been carved by Henry Moore or Marino Marini, are tiny enough to lie on the palm of the hand. The human head which enlarges so well in Plate 13, and is carved of mammoth ivory, is in fact less than 2 inches long. The clay or terracotta figure in Plate 17, in which the emphasis is all on the breast and lower swellings of fertility, stands only a little over four inches (it comes from the mammoth-hunters' station at Dolní Věstonice in Lower Moravia, where excavators have also found little animal figurines in terracotta—bear, for instance, and lion, and woolly rhinoceros; not to mention evidence that the Gravettian hunters of Dolní Věstonice were also given to eating humans).

As Gravettians and Gravettian influence seeped towards the West, so the art of sculpture was added to the pictorial image-making of the cave and shelter peoples, soft stone being used often in place of mammoth ivory or terracotta. The Venus of Willendorf from her Austrian rock-shelter (Plate 25), still the most celebrated of all these progenitive figures, was carved 4⅛ inches high from a scrap of local limestone. The Venus figure from Italy, near Lake Trasimene, in Plate 14, less than 2 inches high (though enlarged to 9 inches), was carved from steatite or soapstone; the 3½-inch figure from the Dordogne in Plate 29 was carved from calcite, the carbonate of lime deposited in caverns. The fine steatopygous fore-and-aft lady from the warm Mediterranean corner of the Balzi Rossi, at Grimaldi, on the frontier between France and Italy (Plate 28), whose shallow cave is passed by everyone who takes the train from Nice or Mentone towards Genoa, is stone instead of mammoth ivory or terracotta (and a mere 2½ inches). Yet ivory carving and carving from bone and antler became part of the western tradition, as in the celebrated female head (just over an inch long) from Brassempouy, which is ivory (Plate 20).

To all these female fertility figures, eastern and western, the phallus of Plate 11 from the Dordogne, carved in bison horn, is a male counterpart.

The Aurignacian culture in the west (and the less important Chatelperronian, which preceded it, in a first fusion with the Mousterian culture of Neanderthal Man) knew conditions moving gradually from warmth and rain, as the ice advanced, to wet and tempestuous and cold. The Gravettian culture flooded into Europe and now superseded or mixed with Aurignacian in conditions increasingly cold and sub-arctic. Mammoth and wild horse were among the chief game of Gravettian hunters; and in the west the combined traditions develop into an art more and more varied and intricate and altogether more remarkable, both in painting and in sculpture.

Painting, drawing, modelling, carving—all are in a way finger arts; as though all of the artist's being, all of his deepest concern, flowed down from him into his finger, more sensitive than tendrils, yet strong and capable; strong, yet precision instruments.

Those tools which extend the fingers or make them capable of dealing more precisely with materials harder than their own flesh and skin, were greatly varied in this long Upper Palæolithic phase of migrations into Europe. Technologically the cultures from Chatelperronian to Magdalenian are grouped as "blade cultures". The first tools and weapons are for clumsy processes, for bruising and crushing and splitting and smashing. Whether it was hafted or held in the hand, an Abbevillian handaxe was a hand-tool, not a finger-tool. The hand took hold of it, or took hold of it by the haft. Crash, and the hand-axe split open a skull; by contrast the finer blades of flint held between finger and thumb, the finer burins or engravers, were moved a millimetre this way, or a millimetre that way, under sensitive control.

The Aurignacians made javelin heads of bone such as quivered in the flesh of the men of the Cougnac cavern: with the little burin of flint the bone points could be notched and decorated (Plate 12).

The Gravettians used small strong knives of flint, curving the tip towards the cutting edge and blunting the back. Add a wooden or bone handle to such a knife (Plate 21) and you have quite clearly the ancestor of our own small knives, which, having pockets, we have improved into the pocket-knife with the blade folding into the handle (which is often made still of slices of deer-horn, as if to remind us of cutting a deer's throat instead of sharpening a pencil). Indeed long before the metal ages, many of our tool-shapes and types were decided in flint for us by our deft-fingered palæolithic ancestors, who used not only knives and burins, but plane-blades, spoke-shaves, awls, etc. (Plate 26), in a whole workshop of "machine tools" or basic tools of flint with which a wider technical armoury of secondary tools and weapons in bone, etc., was fashioned (and then often decorated).

With the sharp point of his burin, the Gravettian upon cavern walls could engrave animals in outline, adding afterwards a painted line or filling the area with paint. With his sharp burin he could engrave animals upon pebbles and small slabs of stone—brown bear (Plate 24), woolly rhinoceros (Plate 26: shown in characteristic position with head down for grazing and grubbing at low semi-arctic vegetation), wild horse (Plate 27, superimposed above engravings of other animals including reindeer).

The Gravettian in Western Europe, taking to caves and shelters and less of a nomad than upon the eastern steppes, now became a painter of considerable virtuosity, matching his pebble and slab engravings with shrine paintings which are well poised, in symbolic images, between ideal forms and natural likenesses. There is still uncertainty and argument about the dating and cultural ascription of the animals in the painted shrine at Lascaux, a cave which everyone should visit while its tawny colours, black and red and brown and yellow and violet, are still fresh and vivid (it is a possibility, I should think a probability, judging from what has happened in other caves such as Font-de-Gaume—Plate 71—, that in fifty years time the bison, the wild cattle, wild horses and red deer of Lascaux will be no more than ghostly presences just discernible upon the rock). The artists of Lascaux succeed with some animals, and fail with others; some animals they present in symbolic life-images, frisky horses in their friskiness, tender-muzzled deer in their tenderness, and in the spideriness of their antlers (Plate 22). Others, such as the huge wild cattle (Plate 22—a huge ox around the three horses) or the bison bulls tail to tail (Plate 23), are images which excite less admiration than wonder. Gravettians in the West carefully buried their dead in caves, often packing them (or their dried bodies?) in red ochre, perhaps as a symbolic blood.

From this stock came most of the hunters of Upper Palæolithic Britain, below the ice-margin; a scanty artless or almost artless population who left their burials in Goat's Hole at Paviland in the Gower Peninsula (" the Red Lady of Paviland ") and in various caves in the Mendip limestone.

Between Gravettian and Magdalenian, between livelier stylization in palæolithic art and its full-blown naturalism, there comes a relatively short phase known as Solutrean, marked by an intrusion of technological ideas from Africa by way of Spain. Solutrean are the leaf flints (Plate 31), thin and carefully worked by pressure-flaking in shapes of leaf-like regularity; and probably Solutrean as well—at any rate they belong to this time-phase of Solutrean technique—are the earliest of the relief sculptures of France; not in caves, but on the face of rock-shelters at the foot of limestone cliffs.

The climate had become more glacial. Herds of wild horses grazed over the cold French plains, which were rich in grass, in the brief summer; and these horses became a principal Solutrean, as they had been a principal Gravettian, concern. Evidence suggests large-scale " drives ", arranged so that horses plunged to death over precipices in the limestone. Solutré itself, the type-site for Solutrean artifacts, near Macon, is a village under the cliffs of a narrow hill ideally formed for such a drive and slaughter. Below the vines which supply the grapes for Pouilly-Fuissé, a huge thickness of horse-bones has been discovered here at Solutré, Gravettian for the most part, with Gravettian burials; and then Solutrean implements.

Elsewhere, on a limestone bulge under a cliff at Mouthiers-sur-Boëme, in Charente, Solutrean sculptors cut (and then coloured) a frieze of mares and stallions a little less than life-size, a stallion covering one of the mares. Elsewhere, they carved ibex, and wild boar and wild oxen—at Le Roc de Sers, also in Charente, for example; and—oxen this time—at the Fourneau-du-diable site near Bourdeilles in the Dordogne, where bull and cow were represented one above the other (Plate 30).

This Solutrean relief sculpture has both prologue and epilogue. It develops out of small, shallow Gravettian rock reliefs; it develops into the grander, deeper, processional reliefs of the Magdalenians. Not very far from Lascaux, down the Vézère and then up one of its tributaries, palæolithic hunters and sculptors utilized overhangs and bulges of limestone which they found exactly to their liking for art and shelter. At one point, higher in the valley, a château—the château of Laussel—stands out on the edge of the cliff. Underneath were found relief carvings—Gravettian—not only the Venus of Laussel, 15¾ inches high, a larger version of the Venus of Willendorf of Plate 25 or the eastern Venus of Plate 17, though she holds in one hand a bison horn; but also a small shallow relief of a man and a woman *in coitu*.

A little way down the valley, at Cap Blanc, a site no less impressive and extraordinary in its way than Lascaux or Altamira, excavators uncovered below a bulge of limestone a frieze of seven horses larger than life. They had been cut in deep relief, then polished, and coloured —as stone sculpture was coloured in the ancient historic civilizations and in the Middle Ages. These and similar carvings were the Magdalenian epilogue.

Small figures in the hand, for nomads upon the move, then reliefs on the rock, still not very large, then friezes polished and coloured but less than life size (the bull in Plate 30—the upper creature—is just short of 14 inches from muzzle to tail): then, last of all, horses in a procession of mare and stallion more than the size of life—here, step after step, we have a progression emphasizing the inheritance which came to the Magdalenians. Or it could be expressed in terms of painting and drawing: scrawls in the clay, hand-stencils on the limestone, outline engravings, coloured outlines, outlines filled rather simply with flat colour—and last of all the Magdalenian grandeurs of shaded polychrome beasts spread across the rock as boldly as a huge fresco of St. Christopher opposite the door of a mediæval church (and with far more life and energy).

The Magdalenians were heirs to the ages, as we say of ourselves. Their situation, as one looks back to them, may not appear enviable.

A corridor stretched from east to west below the ice—and above the Mediterranean. The glacier line reached its limit little north of Moscow, then across Germany round about Berlin, bending upwards to Denmark, and crossing the old lands of the North Sea. Scotland, the North of England, most of Wales were buried below the ice, leaving in our palæolithically provincial corner only the Midlands, some of East Anglia, a strip of South Wales, and the southern counties from Cornwall to Kent, from the Severn across to Essex, as a habitat for man and beast. Along the great corridor of Europe it was either steppe or tundra shading off in the south to forest—though the tundra had its patches of low vegetation and a richer aspect, say, than the modern tundras of Lapland or Russia.

This was the Eskimo world in which the Magdalenians enjoyed their heritage of the cultures of the Upper Palæolithic, fusing, accentuating, adapting, improving, adding elements of their own.

It rather seems that their appearance, in clothing, was no less Eskimo than their world. One thing marking the Magdalenian shelters and home-sites is an abundance of a new and familiar implement—the needle (Plate 33, left), made of bone neatly rubbed down and eyed and pointed. The needle speaks of a stitching (with animal tendons as thread) of closer and cosier garments; and such garments of hide and fur were obviously demanded by the climate of the Last Glaciation which had now come to its bitter climax.

This climax made another change in European life. Local variations apart, the basis of Magdalenian existence became the reindeer, which migrated north and south in vast herds between the ice-country and the woodland into which tundra steppe merged on their southern and more clement fringes. Reindeer was the universal supplier: reindeer was meat, reindeer was fat, it was hide, and tendon; the hard antlers which the stags shed in early winter save the best of all material for a score of essential weapons and tools. For hunting the reindeer Magdalenians invented barbed " harpoons " (Plate 33, right) or barbed spear-heads, appropriately made of this antler of the animal they were turned against. With antler harpoons—a shower of antler harpoons—huntsmen would catch the reindeer in passage, perhaps, above all, at their river crossings. From the slaughtered reindeer the huntsmen would extract the canines, pierce them, decorate them, then wear them as necklaces or pendants, sometimes pairing them in a sexual symbolism (Plate 70).

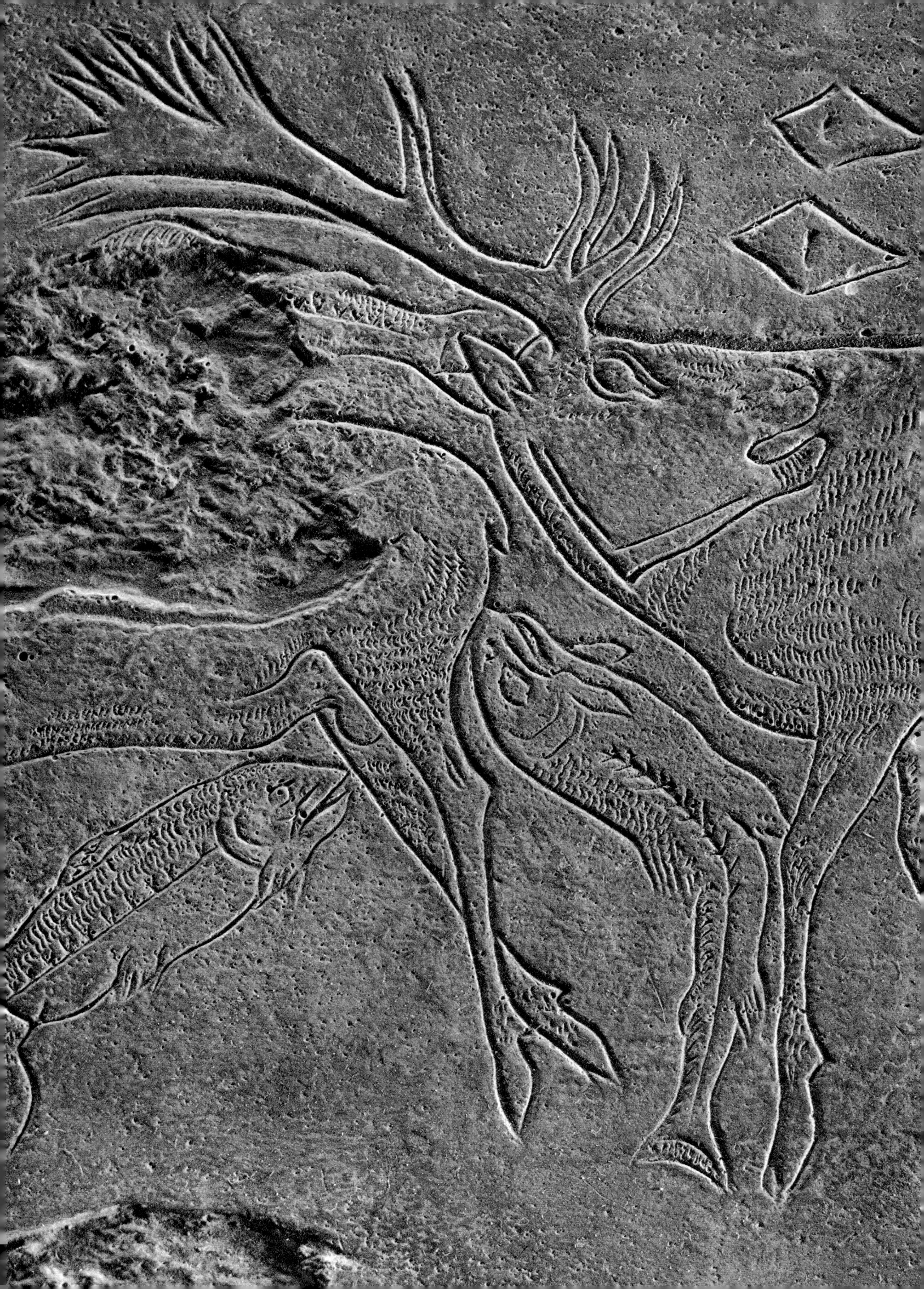

64

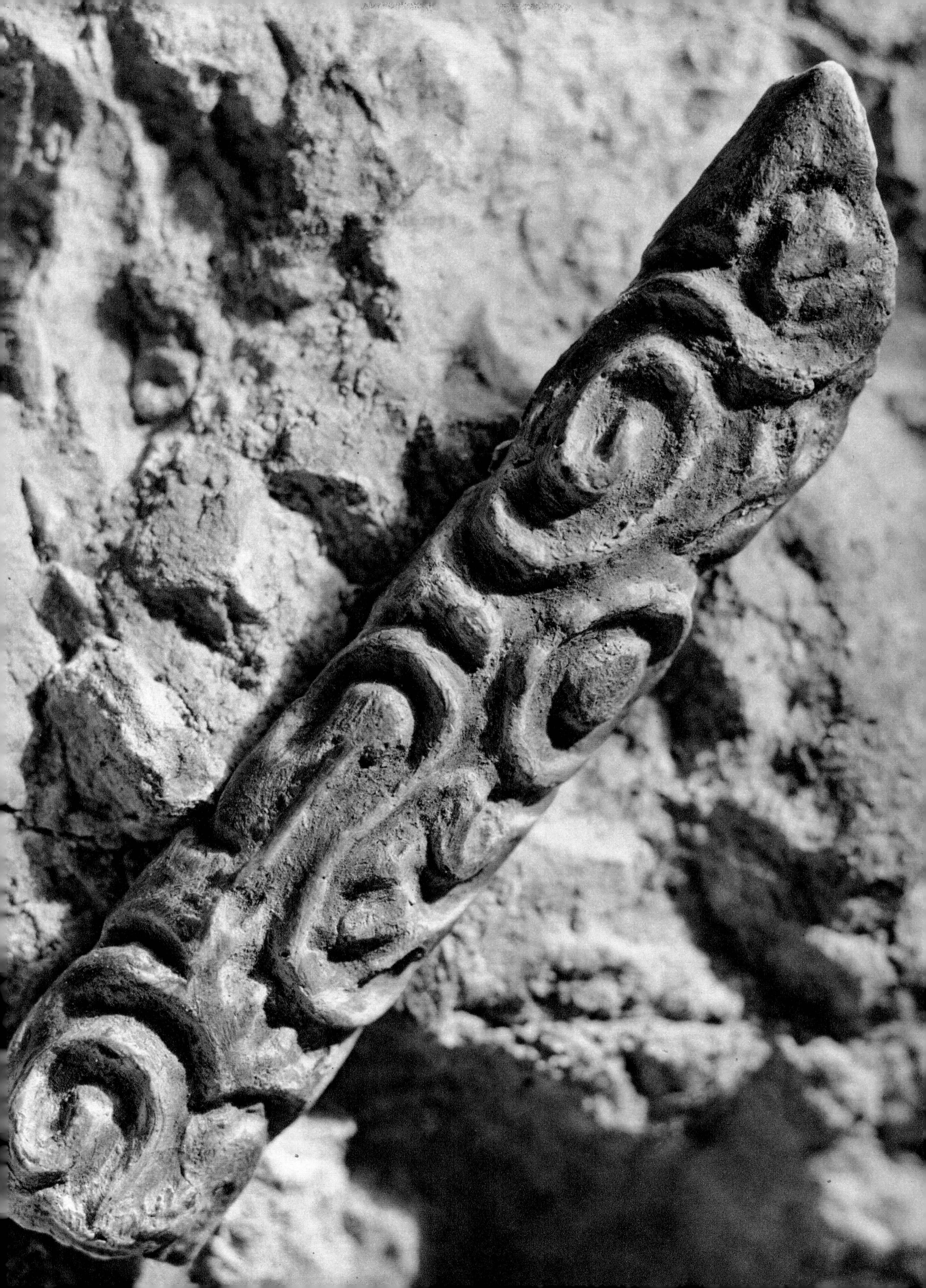

66

67

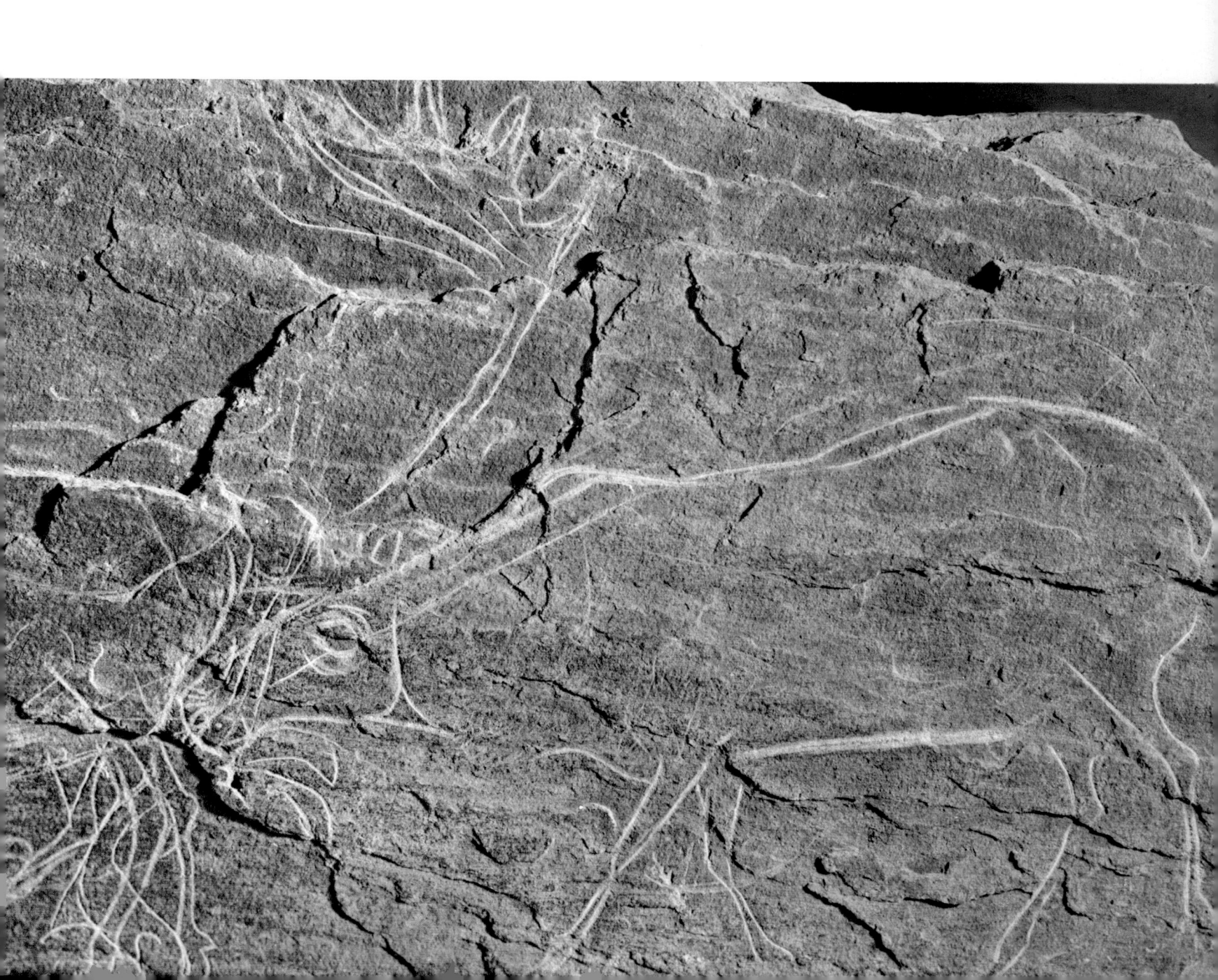

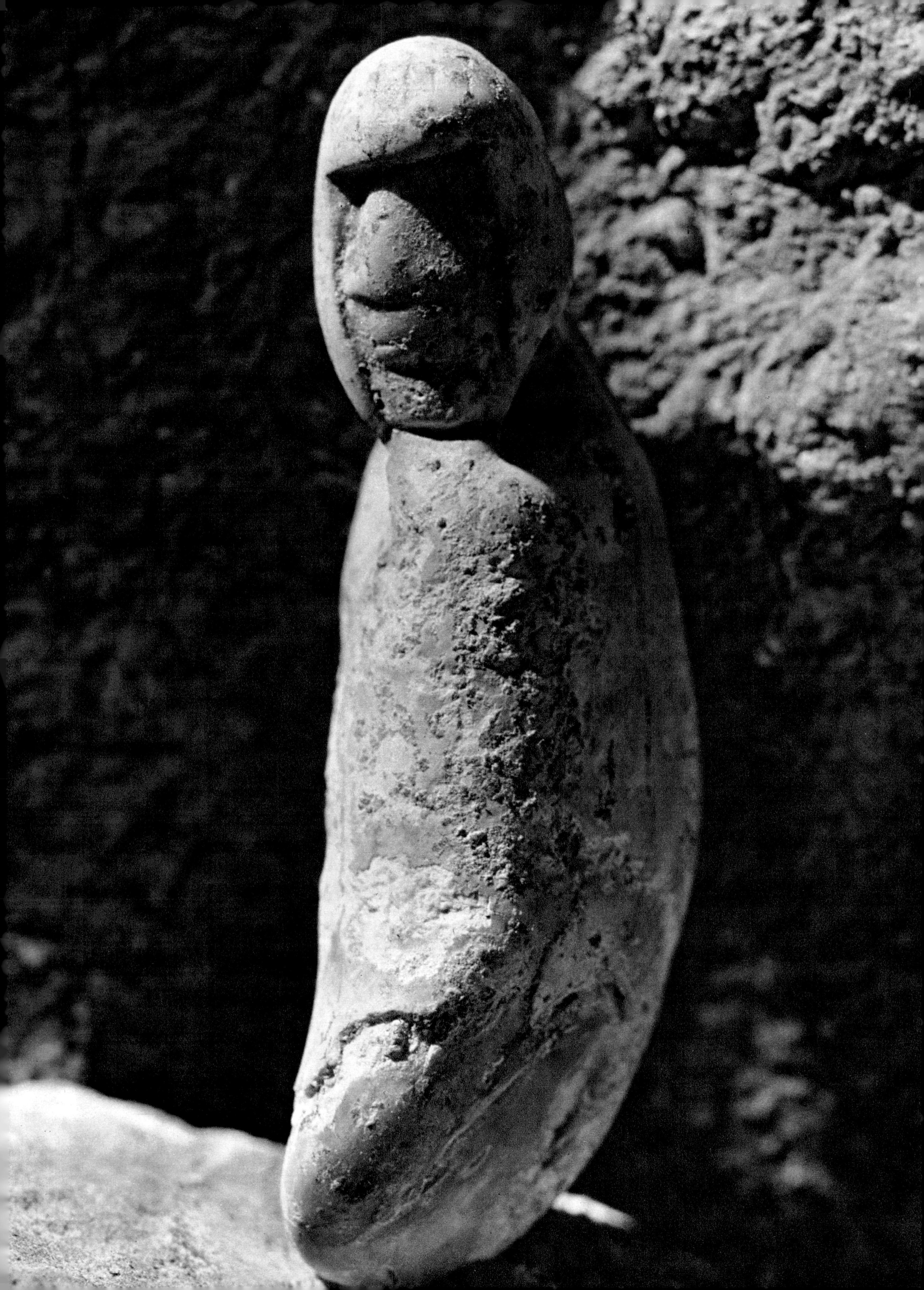

70

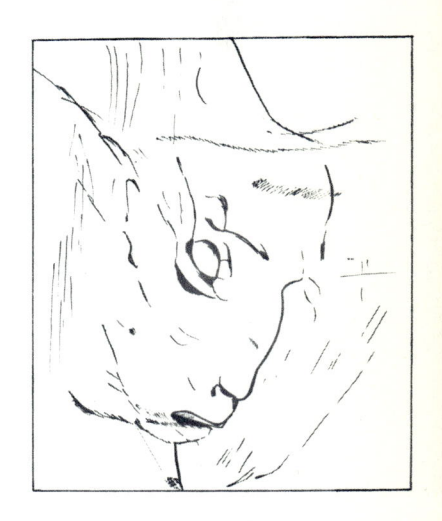

71

72

Antler was the common substance, not only for harpoons, but for notched spear-throwers, with which harpoon or bone-pointed spear fitted against the notch or peg could be thrown further and with more accuracy; also for the curious objects variously explained as arrow-straighteners, thong-softeners, and *bâtons de commandement* or sceptres (Plate 37). These explanations strike me as projections of the material and the romantic fancies. The *bâtons* are commonly found in Magdalenian sites, and seldom show about the hole any of the wear which might argue that they had been tools. No, sceptre is nearer the mark; and since there can hardly have been a supply of " kings " or chieftains to match the great number of these recovered objects, perhaps it would be nearer still to suggest that they were carried in dances, ornamented perhaps with tufts of hair or feathers or other finery. An old and possible and allied suggestion was that they were drumsticks.

The specimen in Plate 37 has been sensibly photographed with a small burin or engraving tool of flint—a tool of the kind which would have been used to give the *bâton* its linear (and probably stylized and meaningful) decoration.

From early times (Plate 32) Magdalenian craftsmen had a gift for ornament, or for ornament and carving combined, in which we can admire an energy derived from the spiritual and practical " at-homeness " in their world. *Bâton*, spear-thrower, harpoon, all these were decorated; and *bâton* and spear-thrower were frequently embellished terminally with carvings of animals—admirable carvings which could be described as samples of ideal form in combination with natural shape, samples of the " concord of pictorial and formal elements " responsible for so much of art's most durable excitement.

The spear-thrower, so to say, extended the arm, as an Abbevillian hand-axe had extended the hand: it gave the arm extra length and an extra joint, it imparted to the spear or harpoon-spear an extra range: natural enough, then, to carve so important a device with images of the beasts it helped to kill—or of beasts which might symbolically add power to the spear thrust—ibex, or reindeer (Plate 38—though this piece is more likely a dagger of reindeer horn than a spear-thrower), or lion or bison (Plates 39 and 44). And if dances had to do with the fertility of man and quarry, with animal kinship, and with success in the hunt, natural enough that the *bâtons* as well (if they were either carried in dances or used as drum-tappers as I have suggested) should have been carved with terminals which range from phalli to the heads of bison (Plate 45); or that along the shafts—as along the shafts of spear-throwers or even along the points of spears—there should be horses, stags, reindeer, fish, etc., engraved in outline.

The sheer lines and bars engraved in series, below an animal (Plate 35), on a harpoon (Plate 33), or on the branches and shaft of a *bâton* (Plate 37), or the scroll decoration along a rod or wand of reindeer antler (Plate 65), were probably conventionalized symbols, as I have mentioned. We may not be able to interpret these symbols with any certainty, though it is no contradiction, and no occurrence without parallel, for a symbolical, conventional art and a naturalistic art to exist side by side.

Also with the Magdalenians, no less than their predecessors, or for that matter their successors in the various cultures of the world, the expressive energy of the sculptor or painter will vary. A relief engraving may seem feeble or commonplace (Plate 43); from another hand a relief on reindeer antler may have the classical composure of the salmon and stags in Plate 63, or a quick sketch may have the tenderness and energy of the reindeer on a scrap of schist in Plate 68. As we have seen, though, a slack interest may also lead to slack or dull images. A bird may seem naïve as a child's drawing (Plate 36), odd human figurines, the woman and the man cut from horse's teeth (Plates 40 and 69), may deserve no particular æsthetic praise; but set against them carvings or drawings of animals which mattered more intensely to the Magdalenian and figured more in his waking life and his dreams, and the contrast may be such as you see in the assured, strong simplifications of an ibex (Plate 35), or of a bison (Plate 42), or of the astonishing figurations of the wild horse, one from Lourdes, from a cave above the grotto of Bernadette's visions (Plate 41), the other from the yawning super-cave of Mas d'Azil, under the Pyrenees (Plate 66).

Both stand comparison with any animal carvings of the world. Enlarge the horse's head (Plate 66) from its actual inch and a-half to the 11 inches of the plate or enlarge it again by as much or by twice as much, and it still retains its monumental "truth", which can only happen when a good artist has concentrated his whole power upon his theme, so that "the elements of form presented by nature are redeemed by art".

Scenes painted or engraved in shelters in Eastern Spain, and a few elsewhere, by artists of the Upper Palæolithic peoples rather more concerned with themselves and their own activities, still picture the game animals with a naturalistic verve denied by the artist to his men and his women—in Plate 72, for example, a scene from one of the few Italian sites, the stag is depicted with an energy of apprehension denied to the humans.

What exactly happened in the cave shrines? No cave after so great a passage of time preserves enough to hint at the full story. One may suspect that each tribe or group had its own shrine, visited at intervals by the artist-shaman, who touched up the paintings or made new ones over the old ones, and by candidates for initiation into tribal knowledge, or into the more specialized knowledge of the shamans. In the Dordogne, Denis Peyrony discovered the original entrance to the painted cave of Bernifal (a mile or two from the great frieze of horses at Cap Blanc): it had been blocked by palæolithic users, as though the caves were visited only at intervals, and were then carefully shut and sealed.

Far inside the caves small stone lamps (Plate 62) have been recovered, in shape much like the bronze or earthenware lamps of classical antiquity. Now and again the millenially old footprints survive in the glacial clay, sometimes casually imprinted (Plate 47), sometimes suggesting a slow dance on the heels. Painted signs and symbols occur, spots and club-shapes in red ochre (Plate 60), track signs, house or hut signs, and others, most of them impossible to interpret, though some beyond reasonable doubt signify traps of one kind and another. In some caves engraving and painting are combined (Plate 71), as one combines drawing and painting, drawing first, painting afterwards, in a modern picture. There are caves primarily full of engravings, such as Les Combarelles (Plate 34), others primarily full of paintings—a distinction due in part to the kind of wall surface.

Niaux (Plates 46-61), in the side of a limestone mountain within view of the Spanish peaks of the Pyrenees, typifies the long dark painful pilgrimage from the outer world of the hunt, past sparkling formations of calcite, past depths, past barriers, past hazards of space and rock and water, through difficulties and through dreads, to the inner silent world of the shrine.

The huntsmen of Niaux seem to have had their home-site in the mouth of a cave on the opposite side of the valley, in the final Magdalenian times. Their artist-shaman did not paint in that late, highly sensual and now celebrated polychrome manner, a glimmer of which is still visible in Font-de-Gaume, near Les Eyzies, and which still glows in the damp Biscayan atmosphere of Altamira. In a style more puritan or provincial he applied black pigment, with a broad vigorous brush-stroke, concentrating, like the Altamira artist-shamans, mostly upon bison (Plates 49, 51, 52, 53, 55, 56, 58), which liked the increasing deciduous forests of the warmer, more oceanic Pyrenean country towards the close of the Upper Palæolithic, but showing by the paintings that he also hunted ibex (Plates 55 and 59) and the horse (Plates 54, 57) on the scrubby and grassy lands down below, as well as the red deer (Plate 50). Here and there in the depths of Niaux there is a quick sketch on the glacial clay—a fish (Plate 48), another bison (Plate 61), stricken also, like its fellows on the wall, with the feathered javelins or harpoons of conservative Magdalenian hunters, who still made little, if any, use—here and everywhere else—of the bow; which was common among huntsmen on the Spanish side of the mountains, who derived it from Africa.

The paintings of Niaux are concentrated in a small roundish lofty "salon noir", half-a-mile underground, in blackness which is palpable and in a silence more than dead which was once faintly, gravely interrupted, one may suppose, by the chanting of the Magdalenian shaman, in his forgotten and irrecoverable language. Here, with no electric light to switch on and off, palæolithic art may be felt in terms which an anthropologist has used of the living art of the Stone Age peoples of Australia—as an expression of palæolithic philosophy in designs which have an aspect of beauty, which reveal æsthetic appreciation, yet are " primarily no attempt to produce the beautiful for its own sake "—an art " first and foremost a ritual activity, correlated with chanting, dancing, acting "; an art which is the visible sign and sacrament of all that palæolithic hunters felt to be the " inner life and meaning, the permanent element, in man and the world, in the present, past, and future."

That it survives at all, that after so many thousand years it can be seen, photographed and gathered into the plates of such an album as this, is miracle enough.

Geoffrey Grigson.

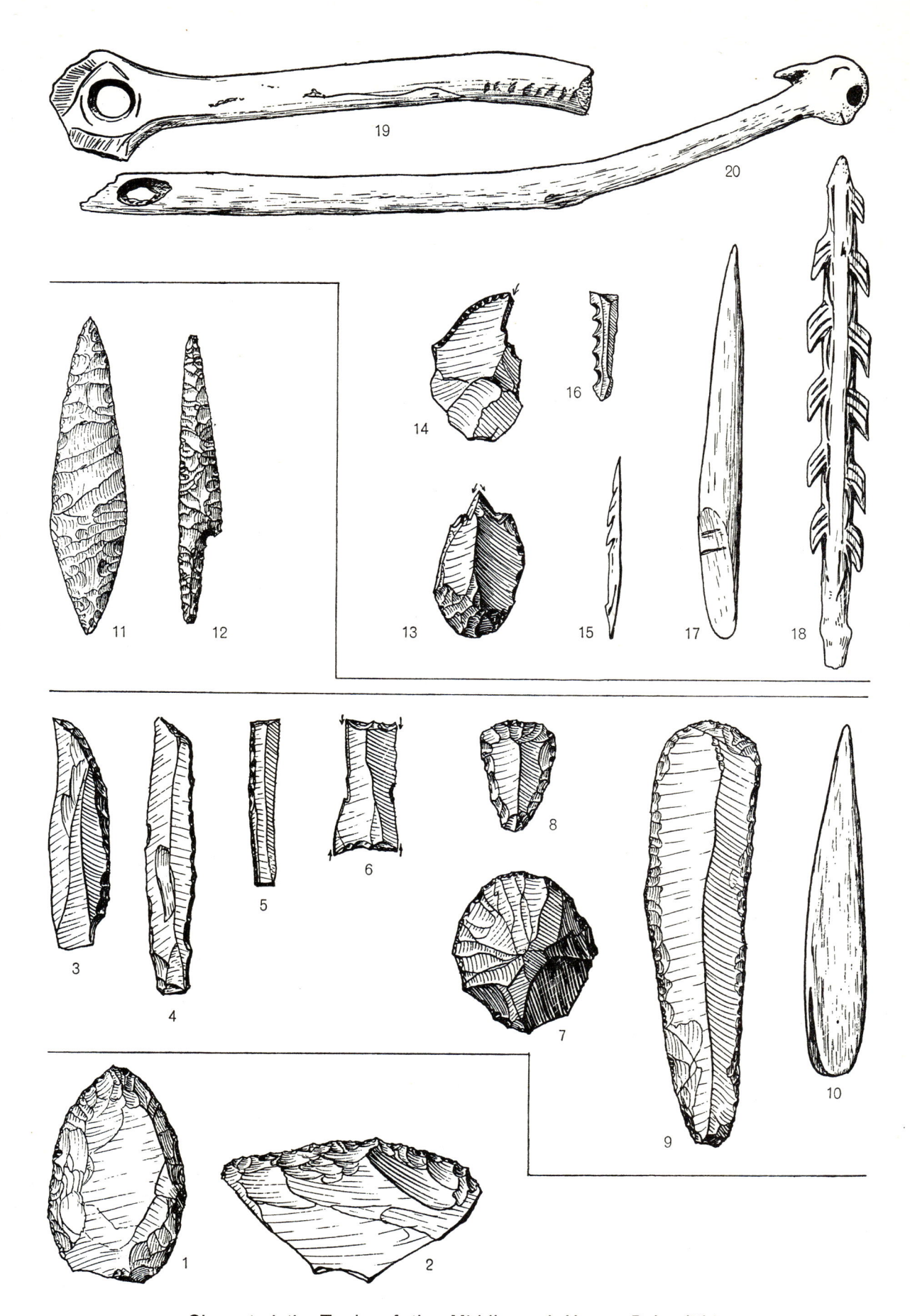

Characteristic Tools of the Middle and Upper Palæolithic

(Scale 1:3, except 19 and 20 which are still more reduced)
Table to be read from bottom to top

Mousterian
1. Mousterian point
2. Side-scraper

Chatelperronian, Aurignacian and Gravettian
3. Chatelperronian knife-point with blunted back edge.
4. & 5. Knife-blades.
6. Noailles graver.
7. Keeled scraper.
8. Scraper.
9. End-scraper and knife.
10. Split-base bone javelin point.

Solutrean
11. "Laurel Leaf" blade
12. Single-shouldered "Willow Leaf" blade.

Magdalenian
13. Graver and end-scraper.
14. Parrot-beak graver.
15. Small harpoon.
16. Blade with denticulated edge.
17. Javelin point.
18. Harpoon.
19. Decorated *Bâton-de-commandement*.
20. Spear-thrower with animal carving.

Chronological and Cultural Framework of Prehistory
applicable particularly to Western Europe

(This very summary table should be read from bottom to top)

Geological period	Climate	Prehistoric period and its cultural characteristics				Human type	Approximate date
Holocene	Temperate modern	**Neolithic**		AGE OF FARMING	Pottery, weaving, sedentary life in villages, agriculture, stock-rearing	Formation of modern races	1800 B.C.
							3500 B.C.
	Temperate damp	**Mesolithic**			Coastal settlement, domestication of the dog		
							7000 B.C.
Pleistocene (Quaternary)	Postglacial (continental)	**Upper Palæolithic**	Magdalenian	AGE OF HUNTER NOMADS	Tools of bone and antler	Appearance in Western Europe of *Homo sapiens*	
			Solutrean Gravettian (Perigordian)		Appearance of art		
	Glacial		Aurignacian Chatelperronian		Blade technique		
							30,000 B.P. (Before Present)
	Cold damp	**Middle Palæolithic**	Mousterian		Ritual interments	Neanderthal Man	
	Variable				Flake technique		
							170,000 B.P.
	Temperate	**Lower Palæolithic**	Acheulian		First occupation of caves	Hominids and prehuman Hominids	
			Abbevillian		Stone tools (bifacial technique)		
	Warm				Employment of fire		500,000 to 1,000,000 B.P.

ABBREVIATIONS: M.A.N. — Musée des Antiquités Nationales, Saint-Germain-en-Laye, France.
M.H.N. — Musée d'Histoire Naturelle, Geneva.
L.G.U.L. — Laboratoire de géologie, University of Lyons.

1. FOLDS IN TERTIARY SCHIST. M.H.N.

2. PLIOCENE LIGNITE. The height of the part shown in the photographs is about 100 mm. Tertiary. From Wetterau, Hesse. British Museum (Natural History), London.

3. ABBEVILLIAN HAND-AXE (bifacial "*coup-de-poing*"). Height 119 mm. From Amiens. Institut d'Anthropologie, University of Geneva.

4. IMPRINT OF A QUATERNARY OAK LEAF. Interglacial. From Cartigny, Geneva. M.H.N.

5. MOUSTERIAN BALLS OF FLINT, which may have been used as bolas stones. From the type site at Le Moustier, in the valley of Rebières, Dordogne. In the collection of Professor Eugène Pittard, Geneva.

6. MOLAR OF MAMMOTH *(ELEPHAS PRIMIGENIUS)*, part of the grinding surface (×2). From Bucharest. M.H.N.

7. MOUSTERIAN PESTLES AND MORTAR (for grinding colours?). From the type site of Le Moustier in the valley of Rebières, Dordogne. From the collection of Professor Eugène Pittard, Geneva.

8. MOUSTERIAN SIDE-SCRAPERS. Idem.

9. PART OF A NEANDERTHAL SKULL, SHOWING THE LOW RECEDING FOREHEAD AND THE LARGE EYE-SOCKETS. La Quina, Charente. From a cast. The original is in the Musée de l'Homme, Paris.

10. PEBBLE AND ROCK scratched in quaternary ice movements M.H.N.

11. STYLIZED MALE MEMBER, in bison horn. Height 178 mm. Gravettian. From the Abri Blanchard, Sergeac, Dordogne. M.A.N.

12. JAVELIN POINTS AND BURIN. Aurignacian. Found in France. M.A.N.

13. HUMAN HEAD, carved in mammoth ivory. Height 47 mm. Gravettian. Dolní Vestonice, Moravia, Czechoslovakia. From a cast.

14. FEMALE FIGURINE OR "VENUS", carved in steatite. Height 37 mm. Probably Gravettian. Found near Lake Trasimene. In the collection of Count Arturo Palma di Cesnola, Florence.

15. HALL OF STALACTITES, Grotte de Cougnac, Lot, with Aurignacian (or Gravettian?) drawing of ibex.

16. PANEL OF AURIGNACIAN OR GRAVETTIAN DRAWINGS IN RED; giant deer with huge antlers *(Cervus megaceros)*, ibex, and a man (in black) pierced with javelins. Grotte de Cougnac, Lot.

17. "VENUS" MODELLED IN CLAY. Height 114 mm. Gravettian. Dolní Vestonice, Moravia, Czechoslovakia. From a cast.

18. WOOD ELEPHANT *(Elephas antiquus)* IN RED OUTLINE, AND A MAN IN BLACK PIERCED WITH JAVELINS. Aurignacian or Gravettian. Grotte de Cougnac, Lot.

19. Detail of the ibex in Plate 16. Grotte de Cougnac, Lot.

20. HEAD OF A FEMALE FIGURINE, carved in mammoth ivory. Height 35 mm. Gravettian. From Brassempouy, Les Landes. M.A.N.

21. GRAVETTIAN KNIFE-BLADES. Maximum length of the blade on the left, 15 mm. From the Durand-Ruel site in the valley of Rebières, Dordogne. In the collection of Professor Eugène Pittard, Geneva.

22. PANEL OF DRAWINGS AND PAINTINGS SUPERIMPOSED. ? Gravettian. In the Grande Salle of Lascaux, Montignac, Dordogne.

23. TWO BISONS BACK TO BACK. ? Gravettian. From the Nave at Lascaux, Montignac, Dordogne.

24. PEBBLE ENGRAVED with a brown bear. Height to the shoulder, 50 mm. Gravettian. From the Abri de la Colombière, Poncin, Ain. L.G.U.L.

25. "VENUS OF WILLENDORF". Height 110 mm. Gravettian. From a cast. The original, carved in limestone, is in the Naturhistorisches Museum, Vienna.

26. PEBBLE ENGRAVED with superimposed figures of woolly rhinoceros and (the other way up) a stag or goat-like creature. Gravettian. From the Abri de la Colombière, Poncin, Ain. Height of rhinoceros to front shoulder, 51 mm. L.G.U.L.

27. PEBBLE ENGRAVED with superimpositions of a stallion, and, the other way up, of reindeer, ibex and felines (?). Height of horse to the mane, 128 mm. Gravettian. Abri de la Colombière, Poncin, Ain. From a cast. The original is in the museum at Bourg, Ain.

28. FEMALE FIGURINE ("The Polchinello") carved in crystalline talc. Height 62 mm. Gravettian. From the Balzi Rossi, Grimaldi, Italy. M.A.N.

29. FEMALE FIGURINE, carved in calcite. Height 92 mm. Gravettian. From the Goulet de Gazelle, Sireuil, Dordogne. M.A.N.

30. BLOCK OF STONE CARVED WITH BOVINES. Length of the lower animal about 360 mm. Solutrean. From Fourneau-du-Diable, Bourdeilles, Dordogne. Museum of Les Eyzies, Dordogne.

31. "LAUREL LEAF" blades in flint. Solutrean. Found in France. M.A.N.

32. **ENGRAVINGS ON A PEBBLE.** Height of the part photographed 190 mm. **Protomagdalenian (according to Peyrony). From Laugerie-Haute, Tayac, Dordogne. Museum of Les Eyzies, Dordogne.**

33. **HARPOON** of reindeer antler with a double row of barbs, and a bone **NEEDLE** with an eye. **Magdalenian. From the type site at La Madeleine, Tursac, Dordogne.**

34. **HEAD OF A YOUNG OR FEMALE IBEX,** engraved on the cavern wall. Length from muzzle to the top of the eye 132 mm. **Magdalenian. Grotte des Combarelles, Tayac, Dordogne.**

35. **CARVING OF AN IBEX** in mammoth ivory. Height from the lower hoof to the tip of the horn 82 mm. **Magdalenian. From Mas d'Azil, Ariège. M.A.N.**

36. **ENGRAVINGS ON A GRITTY STONE SLAB;** head and hindquarters of bison, and a young bird. Maximum length of the bird, 80 mm. **Magdalenian. Puy-de-Lacan, Malemort, Corrèze. From a cast.**

37. **"BÂTON-DE-COMMANDEMENT"** in reindeer antler decorated with (?) stylized fish tails; and a burin. Length of the *bâton*, about 250 mm. **Magdalenian. Laugerie-Basse, Tayac, Dordogne. Musée de l'Homme, Paris.**

38. **LEAPING REINDEER,** carved on the head of a spear-thrower (or haft of dagger?) in reindeer antler. Length from muzzle to hoof, 70 mm. **Laugerie-Basse, Tayac, Dordogne. M.A.N.**

39. **LION (OR HYENA?)** carved on the head of an ivory spear-thrower. Length 110 mm. **Magdalenian. From the type site of La Madeleine, Tursac, Dordogne, M.A.N.**

40. **FEMALE FIGURE** carved from horse's tooth. Height 55 mm. **Magdalenian. From Mas d'Azil, Ariège. M.A.N.**

41. **HORSE** in mammoth ivory. Length 75 mm. **Magdalenian. From Lourdes, Haute-Pyrenées. M.A.N.**

42. **BISON** carved from reindeer antler. Length 108 mm. **Magdalenian. From the type site of La Madeleine, Tursac, Dordogne. M.A.N.**

43. **ENGRAVING OF WOUNDED HINDS.** Distance between the two muzzles, 60 mm. **Magdalenian. Grotte du Chaffaud, Savigné, Vienne. M.A.N.**

44. **BISON LICKING HIS FLANK, DETAIL FROM A RELIEF ON REINDEER ANTLER,** which probably decorated the head of a spear-thrower. Distance from the base of the horn to the end of the muzzle, 36 mm. **Magdalenian. From the type site of La Madeleine, Tursac, Dordogne. M.A.N.**

45. **DETAIL OF ONE OF THE TWO BISONS** decorating the head of a "bâton-de-commandement" in reindeer antler. Distance from the muzzle to the edge of the hole, 67 mm. **Magdalenian. From Laugerie-Basse, Tayac, Dordogne. M.A.N.**

46. to 61. **MAGDALENIAN PAINTINGS AND ENGRAVINGS** in the Grotte de Niaux, near Tarascon, Ariège.

46. **THE GALLERY OF THE STALAGMITE PILLARS,** Niaux.

47. **FOOTPRINTS OF ADOLESCENTS,** in the clay, Niaux.

48. **FISH,** scratched in the clay floor. Niaux. Length about 0.30 m.

49. **WOUNDED BISON,** drawn in black. Niaux. Length about 1.27 m.

50. **LARGE STAG,** drawn in black. Niaux. From the top of the antlers to the muzzle, about 0.39 m.

51. **HEAD AND FOREQUARTERS OF A BISON,** drawn in black Niaux. Length about 1.20 m.

52. **BISON,** drawn in black. Niaux.

53. **DETAIL OF DRAWINGS IN BLACK:** bison, ibex. Niaux. From the tip of the ibex's horn to its muzzle, about 0.33 m.

54. **WILD HORSE,** drawn in black. Niaux. Length about 0.70 m.

55. **PANEL OF DRAWINGS IN BLACK:** wounded bisons and a small ibex pierced with javelins. Niaux. Length of the uppermost bison, about 0.90 m.

56. **HEAD OF A BISON,** drawn in black. Niaux. Distance from the tip of the horns to the muzzle, about 0.39 m.

57. **FOREQUARTERS OF A WILD HORSE,** drawn in black. Niaux. Height to the withers, about 0.80 m.

58. **FOREQUARTERS OF A BISON,** drawn in black. Niaux. Distance from the muzzle to left hoof, about 0.35 m.

59. **IBEX,** drawn in black. Niaux. Length about 0.52 m.

60. **DOTS AND CLAVIFORM SIGNS** painted in red, in the cavern of Niaux.

61. **WOUNDED BISON,** drawn on the clay floor. Niaux. Length 0.58 m.

62. **STONE LAMP AND PENDANT, FLINT SCRAPER AND BURINS, AND HARPOON HEAD, Magdalenian. Musée de l'Homme, Paris.**

63. **DETAIL OF ENGRAVINGS ON CURVED SURFACE OF REINDEER ANTLER** (flattened in plate): stag and salmon Length of the antlers of stag, 49 mm. **Magdalenian. Lorthet, Hautes-Pyrenées, France. M.A.N.**

64. **FELINE (?)** carved in reindeer antler. Height 80 mm. **Magdalenian. Laugerie-Basse, Tayac, Dordogne. M.A.N.**

65. **FRAGMENT OF WAND** in reindeer antler with spiral decoration. Length 76 mm. **Upper Magdalenian. Lespugue, Haute-Garonne. M.A.N.**

66. **HEAD OF A WHINNYING HORSE** in reindeer antler. From the tip of the ear to the end of the muzzle, 45 mm. **Upper Magdalenian. Mas d'Azil, Ariège.**

67. Above, **A SPATULA-SHAPED OBJECT** carved in bone, and an ivory **OBJECT OF UNKNOWN PURPOSE.** Length 95 mm. **Gravettian. Brassempouy, Les Landes. M.A.N.**

68. **REINDEER** carved on a fragment of schist. **Magdalenian. Laugerie-Basse, Tayac, Dordogne. Musée de l'Homme, Paris.**

69. **HUMAN FIGURE** carved from the root of a horse's tooth. Height 45 mm. **Bedeilhac, near Tarascon-sur-Ariège. M.A.N.**

70. **PENDANTS** carved from the abortive canine teeth of reindeer. **Magdalenian. From France. M.A.N.**

71. **HEAD OF A BISON IN PROFILE,** engraved and painted on the cave wall. From the eye to the barb, about 175 mm. **Magdalenian. Font-de-Gaume, Tayac, Dordogne.** The outline drawing above the plate indicates the discernible features.

72. **SCENE WITH HUMAN FIGURES AND ANIMALS** engraved on the cavern wall. Length of stag 310 mm. **Close of the Upper Palæolithic. Addaura, Monte Pellegrino, near Palermo, Sicily.**

Old stone age